quick-method
FAVORITE QUILTS

LEISURE ARTS, INC.
LITTLE ROCK, ARKANSAS

EDITORIAL STAFF

Vice President and Editor-in-Chief:
 Anne Van Wagner Childs
Executive Director: Sandra Graham Case
Executive Editor: Susan Frantz Wiles
Publications Director: Carla Bentley
Creative Art Director: Gloria Bearden
Production Art Director: Melinda Stout

DESIGN
Design Director: Patricia Wallenfang
 Sowers
Senior Designer: Linda Diehl Tiano

PRODUCTION
Managing Editor: Sherry Taylor O'Connor
Technical Writers: Sherry Solida Ford,
 Kathleen Coughran Magee, and Barbara
 McClintock Vechik

EDITORIAL
Associate Editor: Linda L. Trimble
Senior Editorial Writer: Terri Leming
 Davidson
Editorial Associates: Tammi Williamson
 Bradley, Robyn Sheffield-Edwards, and
 Debby Carr
Copy Editor: Laura Lee Weland

ART
Book/Magazine Art Director: Diane M.
 Hugo
Senior Production Artist: M. Katherine
 Yancey
Art Production Assistant: Brent Jones
Photography Stylists: Christina Tiano
 Myers, Sondra Daniel, Karen Smart
 Hall, Aurora Huston, and Connie
 Bennett Basco

BUSINESS STAFF

Publisher: Bruce Akin
Vice President, Finance: Tom Siebenmorgen
Vice President, Retail Sales: Thomas L.
 Carlisle
Retail Sales Director: Richard Tignor
Vice President, Retail Marketing: Pam
 Stebbins
Retail Customer Services Director:
 Margaret Sweetin

Marketing Manager: Russ Barnett
**Executive Director of Marketing and
 Circulation:** Guy A. Crossley
Circulation Manager: Byron L. Taylor
Print Production Manager: Laura Lockhart
Print Production Coordinator: Nancy
 Reddick Lister

Library of Congress Catalog Number 95-78897
Hardcover ISBN 0-942237-60-9
Softcover ISBN 0-942237-61-7

INTRODUCTION

The beloved patterns of yesteryear come alive for busy quilters of today with the timesaving tips found in Quick-Method Favorite Quilts. As you turn the pages, you'll see why we consider these quilts our favorites — their beauty is timeless, and modern methods make them easier than ever to assemble. Whether you're a novice or a proficient quilter, you'll find it a joy to use these latest tools and techniques, along with our convenient shortcuts, to create your own heirloom quilts. Our handy hints even simplify working with templates and appliqués! Thanks to the skill rating assigned to each of our quilts and wall hangings, you can see at a glance which projects are right for you. Even with a full schedule, you can always find time to enjoy our patterns with a variety of smaller, fast-to-stitch designs, including a lap quilt, pillows, decorated clothing, kitchen accessories, and window treatments. From time-tested traditional patterns to our delightful original designs, the projects in this invaluable guide will soon be among the most cherished in your collection!

TABLE OF CONTENTS

STAR-BRIGHT COLLECTION

It's no wonder that quilters have created more than one hundred traditional star patterns — inspiration is ever-present in the broad, open night skies! The fascination with celestial bodies continues today, especially for children, who'll be delighted by the vivid primary hues in our Star-Bright Collection. Twinkling across the quilt is a constellation of red, yellow, and blue LeMoyne Stars and sashing strips that are created using fast, accurate rotary cutting methods. With basic outline and simple decorative quilting, this design is a wish come true.

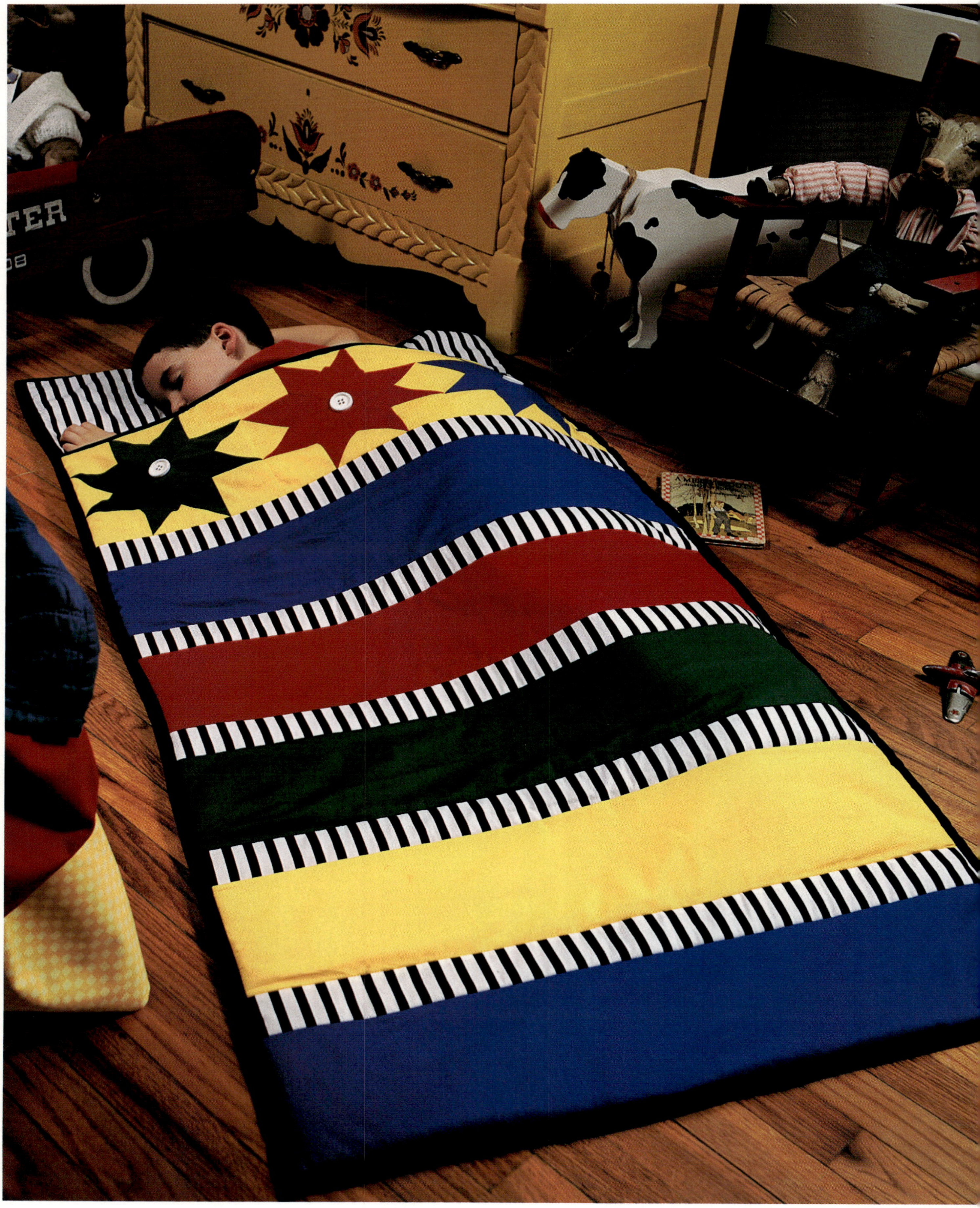

S*lumber parties are full of fun when kids take along our colorful quilted sleeping bag (opposite). It's a dream to sew because the fabric pieces are strip quilted right onto the batting and backing in one simple step. The bottom layer is padded with extra batting for cloudy softness. Accented with colorful buttons, our brilliant wall hanging (below) is fast as a comet to create! Three rotary-cut LeMoyne stars are complemented by an easy-to-piece outer border.*

STAR-BRIGHT QUILT

SKILL LEVEL: 1 2 3 4 5
BLOCK SIZE: 10¼" x 10¼"
QUILT SIZE: 69" x 83"

YARDAGE REQUIREMENTS

Yardage is based on 45"w fabric.

- 3⅞ yds of blue solid
- 2⅝ yds of red solid
- 1¼ yds of yellow solid
  5⅛ yds for backing
  ⅞ yd for binding
  81" x 96" batting

CUTTING OUT THE PIECES

*All measurements include a ¼" seam allowance. Follow
Rotary Cutting, page 144, to cut fabric.*

1. **From blue solid:**
   - Cut 7 strips 3½"w. From these strips, cut
     80 **squares** 3½" x 3½".
   - Cut 3 strips 5½"w. From these strips, cut
     20 **squares** 5½" x 5½". Cut squares twice
     diagonally to make 80 **triangles**.
   - Cut 2 lengthwise strips 6" x 86" for **side
     borders**.
   - Cut 2 lengthwise strips 6" x 62" for **top/bottom
     borders**.

2. **From red solid:**
   - Cut 5 strips 10¾"w. From these strips, cut 49
     sashing strips 3¾" x 10¾".
   - Cut 10 **strips** 2⅝"w.

3. **From yellow solid:**
   - Cut 3 strips 3¾"w. From these strips, cut 30
     sashing squares 3¾" x 3¾".
   - Cut 10 **strips** 2⅝"w.

ASSEMBLING THE QUILT TOP

*Follow **Piecing and Pressing**, page 146, to make quilt top.*

1. Referring to **Fig. 1**, align 45° marking (shown in
   pink) on ruler along lower edge of 1 red **strip**.
   Cut along right edge of ruler to cut 1 end of **strip**
   at a 45° angle. Repeat for remaining red and
   yellow **strips**.

   Fig. 1

   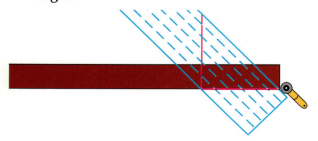

2. Turn 1 cut **strip** 180° on mat and align 45°
   marking on ruler along lower edge of **strip**.
   Align previously cut 45° edge with 2⅝" marking
   on ruler. Cut **strips** at 2⅝" intervals as shown in
   Fig. 2 to make **diamonds**. Cut 80 red **diamonds**
   and 80 yellow **diamonds**.

   Fig. 2

   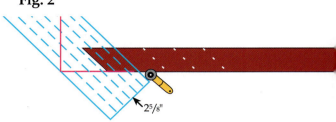

   2⅝"

3. (*Note:* Follow **Working with Diamond Shapes**,
   page 148, for Steps 3 - 6.) Sew 1 red and 1 yellow
   diamond together to make **Unit 1**. Make 80
   Unit 1's.

   Unit 1 (make 80)

4. Sew 2 **Unit 1's** together to make **Unit 2**. Make 40
   Unit 2's.

   Unit 2 (make 40)

5. Sew 2 **Unit 2's** together to make **Unit 3**. Make 20
   Unit 3's.

   Unit 3 (make 20)

6. Sew 1 **Unit 3**, 4 **triangles**, and 4 **squares** together to make **Block**. Make 20 **Blocks**.

Block (make 20)

7. Sew 5 **sashing strips** and 4 **Blocks** together to make **Row**. Make 5 **Rows**.

Row (make 5)

8. Sew 5 **sashing squares** and 4 **sashing strips** together to make **Sashing Row**. Make 6 **Sashing Rows**.

Sashing Row (make 6)

9. Refer to **Quilt Top Diagram**, page 14, to sew **Sashing Rows** and **Rows** together to make center section of quilt top.
10. Follow **Adding Squared Borders**, page 150, to sew **top**, **bottom**, then **side borders** to center section to complete **Quilt Top**.

COMPLETING THE QUILT

1. Follow **Quilting**, page 151, to mark, layer, and quilt, using **Quilting Diagram** as a suggestion. Our quilt is hand quilted using a traditional Baptist Fan design and **Quilting Patterns A** and **B**, page 17.
2. Cut a 30" square of binding fabric. Follow **Binding**, page 155, to bind quilt using 2¹/₂"w bias binding with mitered corners.

Quilting Diagram

13

Quilt Top Diagram

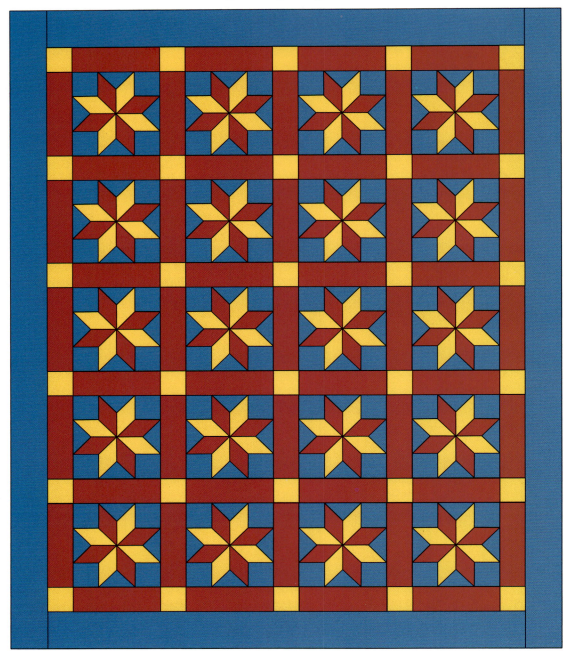

Wall Hanging Top Diagram

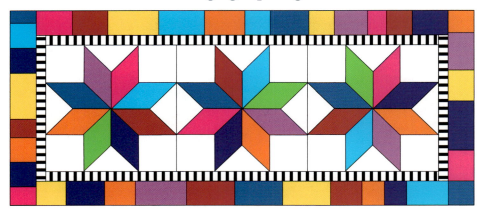

SPARKLING STARS WALL HANGING

SKILL LEVEL: 1 2 **3** 4 5
BLOCK SIZE: 10¼" x 10¼"
WALL HANGING SIZE: 17" x 37"

YARDAGE REQUIREMENTS
Yardage is based on 45"w fabric.

☐ ⅜ yd of white print
▥ ¼ yd of black and white stripe
◪ 10 fat quarters (18" x 22" pieces) of assorted bright prints
⬜ ¾ yd for backing and hanging sleeve
⬜ ⅜ yd for binding
⬜ 21" x 41" batting

You will also need:
  assorted buttons

CUTTING OUT THE PIECES
All measurements include a ¼" seam allowance. Follow Rotary Cutting, page 144, to cut fabric.

1. **From white print:** ☐
   - Cut 1 strip 3½"w. From this strip, cut 12 **squares** 3½" x 3½".
   - Cut 1 strip 5½"w. From this strip, cut 3 squares 5½" x 5½". Cut squares twice diagonally to make 12 **triangles**.
2. **From black and white stripe:** ▥
   - Cut 2 strips 1¼" x 12¼" for **side inner borders**.
   - Cut 2 strips 1¼" x 31¼" for **top/bottom inner borders**.
3. **From assorted bright prints:** ◪
   - Cut 1 **strip** 2⅝" x 18" from 8 different prints.
   - Cut 2½"w pieces that vary in length from 1⅜" to 4½" for **outer border pieces**.

ASSEMBLING THE WALL HANGING TOP
Follow Piecing and Pressing, page 146, to make wall hanging top.

1. Follow Steps 1 and 2 of **Assembling the Quilt Top** for **Star-Bright Quilt**, page 12, to cut 3 **diamonds** from each **strip** (you will need a total of 24 **diamonds**).
2. Using 8 different-colored **diamonds** for each block, follow Steps 3 - 6 of **Assembling the Quilt Top** for **Star-Bright Quilt**, page 12, to make 3 **Blocks**.
3. Refer to **Wall Hanging Top Diagram** to sew **Blocks** together to make center section of wall hanging top.
4. Sew **top**, **bottom**, then **side inner border**s to center section.

5. Sew **outer border pieces** together to make 2 **Top/Bottom Outer Borders** 2½" x 32¾" and 2 **Side Outer Borders** 2½" x 16¼".
6. Sew **Top**, **Bottom**, then **Side Outer Borders** to **inner borders** to complete **Wall Hanging Top**.

COMPLETING THE WALL HANGING
1. Follow **Quilting**, page 151, to mark, layer, and quilt, using **Quilting Diagram** as a suggestion. Our wall hanging is hand quilted.
2. Sew buttons to center of each **Block** and randomly to **Outer Borders.**
3. Follow **Making a Hanging Sleeve**, page 157, to attach hanging sleeve to wall hanging.
4. Follow **Binding**, page 155, to bind wall hanging using 2½"w straight-grain binding with overlapped corners.

Quilting Diagram

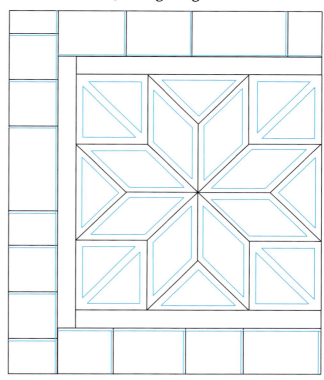

KID'S SLEEPING BAG

SLEEPING BAG SIZE: 32" x 64"

YARDAGE REQUIREMENTS
Yardage is based on 45"w fabric.

▥ 2⅜ yds of black and white stripe
■ 2 yds of black solid
■ 1⅞ yds of red solid
■ ⅝ yd of blue solid
□ ½ yd of yellow solid
■ ⅜ yd of green solid

1¼ yds for binding
1 piece of batting 31¼" x 50¾"
2 pieces of batting 31¼" x 62½"

You will also need:
3 assorted 1" buttons

CUTTING OUT THE PIECES

All measurements include a ¼" seam allowance. Follow **Rotary Cutting***, page 144, to cut fabric.*

1. **From black and white stripe:** ▥
   • Cut 5 **striped pieces** 2½" x 31¼".
   • Cut 1 piece 31¼" x 62½" for **bag back lining**.

2. **From black solid:** ■
   • Cut 1 piece 31¼" x 62½" for **bag back**.

3. **From red solid:** ■
   • Cut 1 **strip** 2⅝"w.
   • Cut 1 piece 31¼" x 50¾" for **bag front lining**.
   • Cut 1 **piece** 6½" x 31¼".

4. **From blue solid:** ■
   • Cut 1 **strip** 2⅝"w.
   • Cut 2 **pieces** 6½" x 31¼".

5. **From yellow solid:** ■
   • Cut 1 strip 3½"w. From this strip, cut 12 **squares** 3½" x 3½".
   • Cut 1 strip 5½"w. From this strip, cut 3 squares 5½" x 5½". Cut squares twice diagonally to make 12 **triangles**.
   • Cut 1 **piece** 6½" x 31¼".

6. **From green solid:** ■
   • Cut 1 **strip** 2⅝"w.
   • Cut 1 **piece** 6½" x 31¼".

MAKING THE SLEEPING BAG

Follow **Piecing and Pressing***, page 146, to make sleeping bag.*

SLEEPING BAG FRONT

1. Follow Steps 1 and 2 of **Assembling the Quilt Top** for **Star-Bright Quilt**, page 12, to cut 8 **diamonds** from each 2⅝"w **strip**.
2. Using 8 matching-colored **diamonds** for each block, follow Steps 3 - 6 of **Assembling the Quilt Top** for **Star-Bright Quilt**, page 12, to make 3 **Blocks**.
3. Sew **Blocks** together to make **Star Panel**.

Star Panel

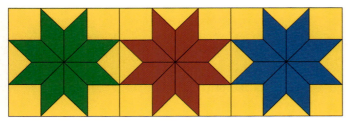

4. To strip quilt bag front, place **bag front lining** wrong side up on a flat surface. Matching edges, place 31¼" x 50¾" batting piece on top of lining. Referring to **Fig. 1**, place 1 blue 6½"w **piece** right side up along bottom edge of batting; pin in place

Fig. 1

5. Referring to **Fig. 2**, place 1 **striped piece** right side down along top edge of blue **piece**, matching long edges. Stitch along top long edge through all layers (**Fig. 2**). Open **striped piece** and press (**Fig. 3**).

Fig. 2

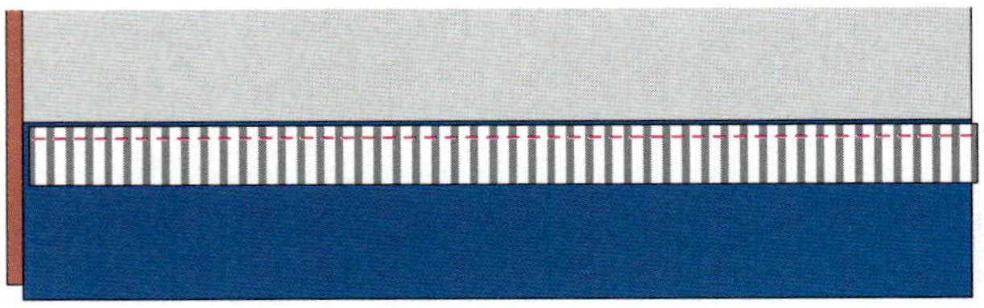

Fig. 3

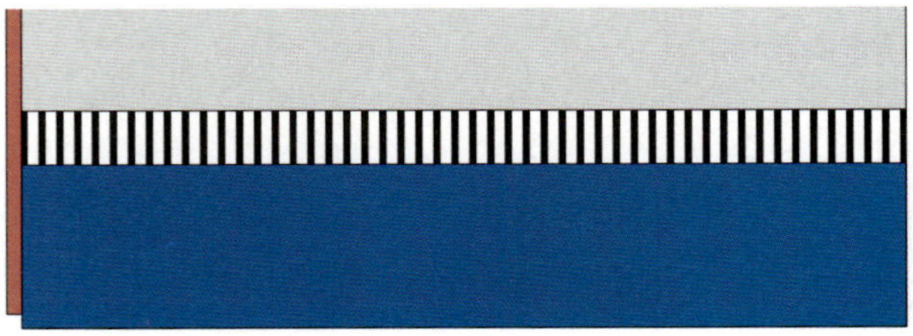

6. Referring to **Sleeping Bag Front Diagram**, repeat Step 5 with remaining 6½"w **pieces**, **striped pieces**, and **Star Panel** to make **Sleeping Bag Front**.
7. Cut a 28" square of binding fabric. Set aside for Step 2 of **Completing the Sleeping Bag**.
8. Cut a 2½" x 36" bias strip from remaining binding fabric. Press bias strip in half lengthwise with wrong sides together. Matching raw edges, sew binding to top edge of **Star Panel**. Fold over to lining and blindstitch in place.
9. Sew 1 button to center of each **Block** to complete **Sleeping Bag Front**.

SLEEPING BAG BACK

1. Beginning at 1 short edge (top), follow **Marking Quilting Lines**, page 152, to mark horizontal lines at 8" intervals on right side of **bag back**.
2. Place **bag back lining** wrong side up on a flat surface. Matching edges, place both 31¼" x 62½

batting pieces, then **bag back** right side up on top of **bag back lining**. Baste in place.

3. Sew along marked lines through all layers to complete **Sleeping Bag Back**.

COMPLETING THE SLEEPING BAG

1. Place **Sleeping Bag Back**, lining side up, on a flat surface. Place **Sleeping Bag Front** on top with bottom edges matching. Baste front and back together along side and bottom edges.

2. Using 28" square of binding fabric and a 1/2" seam allowance, follow **Binding**, page 155, to bind sleeping bag with 3 1/2"w bias binding with mitered corners.

Sleeping Bag Front Diagram

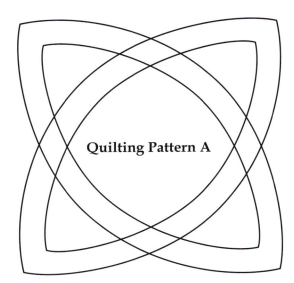

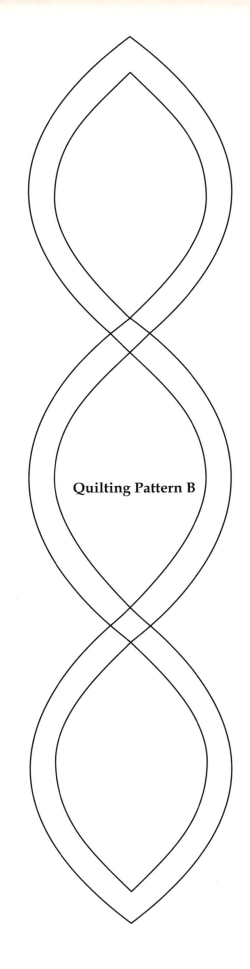

Quilting Pattern B

Quilting Pattern A

BURGOYNE SURROUNDED

The Burgoyne Surrounded design, first published around 1890, recalls the famous Revolutionary War battle in which a small force of valiant Americans surrounded British General John Burgoyne and his troops, forcing their surrender. Also known as Wheel of Fortune and Road to California, our majestic quilt is pieced in the classic red-on-white color scheme by which the pattern is known. But instead of using tedious templates, we've updated traditional methods by using a combination of easy strip piecing and unit piecing to create the dramatic design. Simple-to-mark grid quilting and contrasting binding provide a triumphant finish.

BURGOYNE SURROUNDED QUILT

SKILL LEVEL: 1 2 3 4 5
BLOCK SIZE: 15" x 15"
QUILT SIZE: 81" x 99"

YARDAGE REQUIREMENTS

Yardage is based on 45"w fabric.

☐ 7⅜ yds of white solid
■ 2½ yds of red solid
  7½ yds for backing
  1 yd for binding
  90" x 108" batting

CUTTING OUT THE PIECES

All measurements include a ¼" seam allowance. Follow **Rotary Cutting**, *page 144, to cut fabric.*

1. **From white solid:** ☐
   - Cut 8 **wide strips** 2½"w.
   - Cut 28 **narrow strips** 1½"w.
   - Cut 5 strips 15½"w. From these strips, cut 49 **sashing strips** 15½" x 3½".
   - Cut 2 lengthwise strips 3" x 102" for **side borders**.
   - Cut 2 lengthwise strips 3" x 79" for **top/bottom borders**.
   - From remaining fabric width, cut 16 crosswise strips 3½"w. From these strips, cut 80 **large rectangles** 3½" x 5½".
   - From remaining fabric width, cut 20 crosswise strips 2½"w. From these strips, cut 160 **small rectangles** 2½" x 3½".

2. **From red solid:** ■
   - Cut 12 **wide strips** 2½"w.
   - Cut 30 **narrow strips** 1½"w.

ASSEMBLING THE QUILT TOP

Follow **Piecing and Pressing**, *page 146, to make quilt top.*

1. Sew 1 **narrow** and 2 **wide strips** together to make **Strip Set A**. Make 6 **Strip Set A's**. Cut across **Strip Set A's** at 2½" intervals to make 40 **Unit 1's**. Cut across remaining **Strip Set A's** at 1½" intervals to make 80 **Unit 2's**.

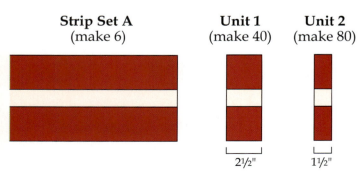

Strip Set A (make 6)   **Unit 1** (make 40)   **Unit 2** (make 80)

2½"   1½"

2. Sew 1 **narrow** and 2 **wide strips** together to make **Strip Set B**. Make 4 **Strip Set B's**. Cut across **Strip Set B's** at 1½" intervals to make 100 **Unit 3's**.

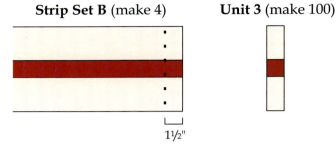

Strip Set B (make 4)   **Unit 3 (make 100)**

1½"

3. Sew 2 **Unit 1's** and 1 **Unit 3** together to make **Unit 4**. Make 20 **Unit 4's**.

Unit 4 (make 20)

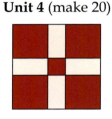

4. Sew 1 **Unit 2** and 1 **Unit 3** together to make **Unit 5**. Make 80 **Unit 5's**.

Unit 5 (make 80)

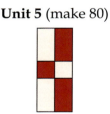

5. Sew 3 **narrow strips** together to make **Strip Set C**. Make 8 **Strip Set C's**. Cut across **Strip Set C's** at 1½" intervals to make 220 **Unit 6's**.

Strip Set C (make 8)   **Unit 6 (make 220)**

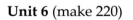

1½"

Sew 3 **narrow strips** together to make **Strip Set D**. Make 4 **Strip Set D's**. Cut across **Strip Set D's** at 1½" intervals to make 110 **Unit 7's**.

Strip Set D (make 4)

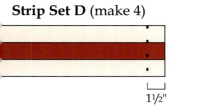

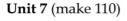

1½"

Unit 7 (make 110)

Sew 2 **Unit 6's** and 1 **Unit 7** together to make **Unit 8**. Make 110 **Unit 8's**.

Unit 8 (make 110)

Sew 2 **narrow strips** together to make **Strip Set E**. Make 6 **Strip Set E's**. Cut across **Strip Set E's** at 1½" intervals to make 160 **Unit 9's**.

Strip Set E (make 6)

1½"

Unit 9 (make 160)

Sew 2 **Unit 9's** together to make **Unit 10**. Make 80 **Unit 10's**.

Unit 10 (make 80)

0. Sew 1 **Unit 5** and 1 **large rectangle** together to make **Unit 11**. Make 80 **Unit 11's**.

Unit 11 (make 80)

11. Sew 1 **Unit 10**, 2 **small rectangles**, and 1 **Unit 8** together to make **Unit 12**. Make 80 **Unit 12's**. (Set aside remaining **Unit 8's** to use in Step 16.)

Unit 12 (make 80)

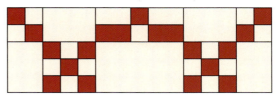

12. Sew 1 **Unit 11** and 2 **Unit 12's** together to make **Unit 13**. Make 40 **Unit 13's**.

Unit 13 (make 40)

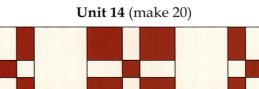

13. Sew 2 **Unit 11's** and 1 **Unit 4** together to make **Unit 14**. Make 20 **Unit 14's**.

Unit 14 (make 20)

14. Sew 2 **Unit 13's** and 1 **Unit 14** together to make **Block**. Make 20 **Blocks**.

Block (make 20)

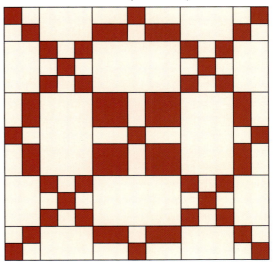

15. Sew 5 **sashing strips** and 4 **Blocks** together to make **Row**. Make 5 **Rows**.

Row (make 5)

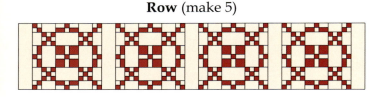

16. Sew 5 **Unit 8's** and 4 **sashing strips** together to make **Sashing Row**. Make 6 **Sashing Rows**.

Sashing Row (make 6)

17. Referring to **Quilt Top Diagram**, sew **Sashing Rows** and **Rows** together to make center section of quilt top.
18. Follow **Adding Squared Borders**, page 150, to sew **top**, **bottom**, then **side borders** to center section to complete **Quilt Top**.

COMPLETING THE QUILT

1. Follow **Quilting**, page 151, to mark, layer, and quilt, using **Quilting Diagram** as a suggestion. Our quilt is hand quilted.
2. Cut a 34" square of binding fabric. Follow **Binding**, page 155, to bind quilt using 2¹/₂"w bias binding with mitered corners.

Quilting Diagram

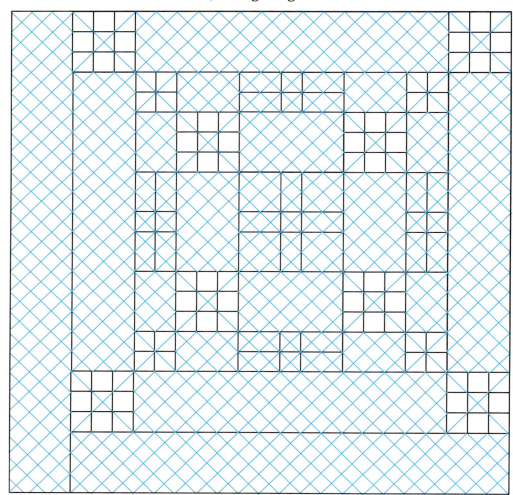

Quilt Top Diagram

SOFT & SWEET PILLOWS

When you have the quilting "bug" but don't want to undertake a large project, pillows are ideal for sampling your favorite patterns. Most quilt blocks are just the right size for comfy cushions! You can mix and match motifs from any of our collections — such as the LeMoyne Star from our Star-Bright quilt, the appliquéd block from our Pastel Posies quilt, and the Ohio Star block from the O My Stars! quilt. Simply piece them using coordinating fabrics and arrange them together for a decorator's touch! Whether finished with a crisp edge, a charming ruffle, or elegant welting, the pillows will create a treasury of quilted keepsakes to accent your home.

OHIO STAR PILLOW

PILLOW SIZE: 15" x 15" (including ruffle)

YARDAGE REQUIREMENTS

Yardage is based on 45"w fabric.

- ½ yd of yellow print
- ½ yd of green solid
- ¼ yd of green print
- ¼ yd of pink print
  14" x 14" pillow top backing
  10" x 10" pillow back
  1¼ yds of ⅛" cord for welting
  14" x 14" batting

You will also need:
polyester fiberfill

CUTTING OUT THE PIECES

All measurements include a ¼" seam allowance. Follow Rotary Cutting, page 144, to cut fabric.

1. **From yellow print:**
   - Cut 1 **small rectangle** 3½" x 5" for triangle-squares.
   - Cut 1 **center square** 1½" x 1½".
   - Cut 1 **strip** 5½" x 80" for ruffle, pieced as necessary.

2. **From green solid:**
   - Cut 1 **bias strip** 1¼" x 45" for welting, pieced as necessary.

3. **From green print:**
   - Cut 1 **small rectangle** 3½" x 5" for triangle-squares.
   - Cut 4 **very small squares** 1½" x 1½".
   - Cut 1 **large rectangle** 6" x 10" for triangle-squares.
   - Cut 4 **medium squares** 3⅝" x 3⅝".

4. **From pink print:**
   - Cut 1 **large rectangle** 6" x 10" for triangle-squares.

MAKING THE PILLOW

Follow Piecing and Pressing, page 146, to make pillow.

1. Using yellow and green **small rectangles**, **very small squares**, and **center square**, follow Steps 1 - 3 of **Assembling the Quilt Top** for **O My Stars! Quilt**, page 33, to make **Small Ohio Star**.

2. Using green and pink **large rectangles**, **medium squares**, and **Small Ohio Star**, follow Steps 4 - 6 of **Assembling the Quilt Top** for **O My Stars! Quilt**, page 33, to make **Large Ohio Star** for pillow top.

Large Ohio Star (make 1)

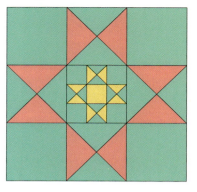

3. Follow **Quilting**, page 151, to mark, layer, and quilt, using **Quilting Diagram**, page 39, as a suggestion. Our pillow top is hand quilted.
4. Follow **Pillow Finishing**, page 158, to complete pillow with welting and a 2½"w ruffle.

LeMOYNE STAR PILLOW

PILLOW SIZE: 17" x 17"

YARDAGE REQUIREMENTS

Yardage is based on 45"w fabric.

- ¼ yd of green solid
- ¼ yd of large yellow print
- scraps of 8 assorted pink and yellow prints
  21" x 21" pillow top backing
  18" x 18" pillow back
  21" x 21" batting

You will also need:
polyester fiberfill
¾" button

CUTTING OUT THE PIECES

All measurements include a ¼" seam allowance. Follow Rotary Cutting, page 144, to cut fabric.

1. **From green solid:**
   - Cut 4 **border squares** 3⅞" x 3⅞".
   - Cut 4 **squares** 3½" x 3½".
   - Cut 1 square 5½" x 5½". Cut square twice diagonally to make 4 **triangles**.

2. **From large yellow print:**
   - Cut 4 **border strips** 3⅞" x 10¾".

3. **From scraps of assorted pink and yellow prints:**
   - From each scrap, cut a **rectangle** 2⅝" x 6½".

MAKING THE PILLOW

Follow Piecing and Pressing, page 146, to make pillow.

- Follow Steps 1 and 2 of **Assembling the Quilt Top** for **Star-Bright Quilt**, page 12, to cut 1 **diamond** from each **rectangle**.
- Follow Steps 3 - 6 of **Assembling the Quilt Top** for **Star-Bright Quilt**, page 12, to make 1 **Block**.

Block (make 1)

- Sew **border strips** to left and right edges of **Block**.
- Sew 1 **border square** to each end of remaining **border strips**; sew **border strips** to top and bottom of **Block** to make pillow top.
- Follow **Quilting**, page 151, to mark, layer, and quilt, using **Quilting Diagram**, page 13, as a suggestion. Our pillow top is hand quilted using **Quilting Patterns A** and **B**, page 17.
- Sew button to pillow top.
- Follow **Pillow Finishing**, page 158, to complete pillow.

FLORAL APPLIQUÉ PILLOW

PILLOW SIZE: 14" x 14"

YARDAGE REQUIREMENTS

Yardage is based on 45"w fabric.

- ³/₈ yd of yellow check
- ¹/₂ yd of green solid
- ¹/₄ yd of pink check
- ¹/₈ yd of small yellow print
- scraps of pink and yellow prints for appliqué
  17" x 17" pillow top backing
  13¹/₂" x 13¹/₂" pillow back
  17" x 17" batting

You will also need:
polyester fiberfill
transparent monofilament thread for appliqué
paper-backed fusible web

CUTTING OUT THE PIECES

All measurements include a ¼" seam allowance. Follow Rotary Cutting, page 144, to cut fabric unless otherwise indicated.

1. For binding, cut 1 bias strip 2¹/₂" x 66" from green solid, pieced as necessary. Press in half lengthwise with wrong sides together.
2. Cut 4 **border strips** 3" x 8¹/₂" from green solid.
3. Cut 4 **border squares** 3" x 3" from small yellow print.
4. Cut 1 **large square** 9" x 9" from yellow check.
5. Cut 4 **medium squares** 3¹/₂" x 3¹/₂" from pink check.
6. Use patterns, page 66, and follow Steps 1 - 3 of **Invisible Appliqué**, page 148, to cut the following:
   - 1 **Large Circle** from pink print scrap
   - 1 **Small Circle** from yellow print scrap
   - 1 **Leaf** from green solid
   - 1 **Stem** from green solid

MAKING THE PILLOW

Follow Piecing and Pressing, page 146, to make pillow.

1. Follow Steps 1 and 2 of **Assembling the Quilt Top** for **Pastel Posies Quilt**, page 64, to make 1 **Block A**.

Block A (make 1)

2. Sew **border strips** to left and right edges of **Block A**.
3. Sew 1 **border square** to each end of remaining **border strips**; sew border strips to top and bottom of **Block A** to make pillow top.
4. Follow **Quilting**, page 151, to mark, layer, and quilt, using **Quilting Diagram**, page 65, as a suggestion. Our pillow top is hand quilted.
5. Trim batting and backing even with pillow top. Place pillow top and pillow back wrong sides together; sew pieces together using a ¹/₄" seam allowance and leaving an opening for stuffing. Stuff pillow with fiberfill and sew opening closed.
6. Follow **Attaching Binding with Mitered Corners**, page 156, to bind pillow edges.

O MY STARS! COLLECTION

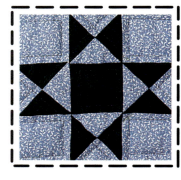

Intricate medallion quilts were among the most prized possessions of Colonial women. George Washington's mother recognized the value of her blue-and-white masterpiece by making special provisions for it in her will. Creating your own heirloom is a joy with our O My Stars! quilt, which features an exquisite Feathered Star surrounded by a series of Wild Goose, Ohio Star, and Delectable Mountains borders. To simplify the quilt, we pieced each design element separately and then used an easy-to-follow diagram to assemble the sections. We also used time-saving techniques, such as a grid method for making the triangle-squares and a "sew-and-flip" system for creating the Wild Goose units.

Making beautiful bedroom accents is easy when you borrow elements from
our O My Stars! quilt. The central medallion of the quilt is the perfect size for
a heavenly wall hanging (below). A series of simple borders and basic quilting
showcase the Feathered Star. Give your room a bright outlook with our Ohio Star
valance and Wild Goose curtain tiebacks (opposite). The top and bottom
borders of the valance double as handy casings for effortless mounting.

O MY STARS! QUILT

SKILL LEVEL: 1 2 3 4 5
QUILT SIZE: 89" x 95"

To simplify construction of this quilt, we grouped its elements into specific sections. Please refer to Assembly Diagram, page 37, for section names when selecting fabrics and while assembling quilt top.

YARDAGE REQUIREMENTS
Yardage is based on 45"w fabric.

- ☐ 2⅞ yds **total** of very light blue prints:
  1⅜ yds for Feathered Star and Border #1
  1½ yds for Border #3
- ☐ 1¾ yds of light blue print for Feathered Star and Border #2
- ☐ 8⅛ yds **total** of medium blue prints:
  1⅝ yds for Feathered Star and Border #3
  4⅛ yds for Border #1 and Outer Border
  2 yds for Border #2
  ⅜ yd for Inner Border
- ☐ 2½ yds of dark blue print for Border #3
- ☐ 1¾ yds of dark blue solid for Border #1 and Border #2
  8¼ yds for backing
  1 yd for binding
  120" x 120" batting

CUTTING OUT THE PIECES
All measurements include a ¼" seam allowance. Follow Rotary Cutting, page 144, to cut fabric unless otherwise indicated. Label and group all pieces for each section into individual stacks.

1. **From very light blue prints:** ☐

(for Feathered Star)
- Cut 1 square 13⅛" x 13⅛". Cut square twice diagonally to make 4 **large triangles**.
- Cut 1 **square** 11" x 11" for triangle-square B's.
- Cut 2 **large rectangles** 6" x 10" for large triangle-squares and triangle-square A's.
- Cut 4 **large squares** 6⅛" x 6⅛".
- Cut 1 **small rectangle** 4" x 6" for small triangle-squares.
- Cut 4 **medium squares** 3⅝" x 3⅝".
- Cut 4 **very small squares** 1½" x 1½".
- Cut 4 squares 2⅛" x 2⅛". Cut squares once diagonally to make 8 **triangle A's**.
- Cut 4 squares 2³⁄₁₆" x 2³⁄₁₆". Cut squares once diagonally to make 8 **triangle B's**.

(for Border #1)
- Cut 8 strips 2"w. From these strips, cut 160 **squares** 2" x 2".

(for Border #3)
- Cut 2 strips 8¾"w. From these strips, cut 5 squares 8¾" x 8¾". Cut squares twice diagonally to make 20 **large triangles**.

- Cut 1 strip 2⅝"w. From this strip, cut 12 squares 2⅝" x 2⅝". Cut squares once diagonally to make 24 **medium triangles**.
- Cut 2 **rectangles** 17" x 20" for triangle-squares.
- Cut 2 squares 9⅝" x 9⅝". Cut squares once diagonally to make 4 **corner triangles**.
- Cut 2 squares 2⅛" x 2⅛". Cut squares once diagonally to make 4 **small triangles**.

2. **From light blue print:** ☐

(for Feathered Star)
- Cut 1 **large rectangle** 6" x 10" for triangle-square A's.
- Cut 1 **square** 11" x 11" for triangle-square B's.
- Cut 1 **small rectangle** 4" x 6" for small triangle-squares.
- Cut 1 **center square** 1½" x 1½".
- Cut 4 **small squares** 1¾" x 1¾".
- Cut 2 squares 2³⁄₁₆" x 2³⁄₁₆". Cut squares once diagonally to make 4 **triangle B's**.

(for Border #2)
- Cut 8 strips 2½"w. From these strips, cut 128 **squares** 2½" x 2½".
- Cut 2 **rectangles** 18" x 24" for triangle-squares.

3. **From medium blue prints:** ☐

(for Feathered Star)
- Cut 1 **large rectangle** 6" x 10" for large triangle-squares.
- Cut 4 squares 4⅝" x 4⅝". Cut squares once diagonally to make 8 **medium triangles**.
- Use pattern, page 37, and follow **Template Cutting**, page 146, to cut 8 **diamonds** (4 in reverse).

(for Inner Border)
- Cut 4 **inner border strips** 2⅜" x 31".

(for Border #1)
- Cut 4 lengthwise **border #1 strips** 5" x 46".

(for Border #2)
- Cut 4 lengthwise **border #2 strips** 3½" x 64".

(for Border #3)
- Cut 2 strips 8¾"w. From these strips, cut 6 squares 8¾" x 8¾". Cut squares twice diagonally to make 24 **large triangles**.
- Cut 1 strip 2⅝"w. From this strip, cut 10 squares 2⅝" x 2⅝". Cut squares once diagonally to make 20 **medium triangles**.
- Cut 4 squares 2⅛" x 2⅛". Cut squares once diagonally to make 8 **small triangles**.
- Cut 2 **rectangles** 17" x 20" for triangle-squares.

(for Outer Border)
- Cut 1 lengthwise **top outer border strip** 12½" x 92".
- Cut 1 lengthwise **bottom outer border strip** 6½" x 92".
- Cut 2 lengthwise **side outer border strips** 6½" x 80".

From dark blue print:

(or Border #3)
- Cut 2 lengthwise **top/bottom border #3 strips** 3½" x 80".
- Cut 2 lengthwise **side border #3 strips** 3½" x 74".

From dark blue solid: ■

(or Border #1)
- Cut 4 strips 3½"w. From these strips, cut 80 **rectangles** 2" x 3½".

(or Border #2)
- Cut 2 strips 2½"w. From these strips, cut 32 **center squares** 2½" x 2½".
- Cut 2 **rectangles** 18" x 24" for triangle-squares.

ASSEMBLING THE QUILT TOP

Follow Piecing and Pressing, page 146, to make quilt top.

FEATHERED STAR and INNER BORDER

1. To make small triangle-squares, place very light blue and light blue **small rectangles** right sides together. Referring to **Fig. 1**, follow **Making Triangle-Squares**, page 147, to make a total of 4 **small triangle-squares**.

Fig. 1

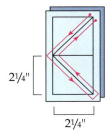

small triangle-square (make 4)

2. Referring to **Fig. 2**, place 2 **small triangle-squares** right sides and opposite colors together, matching seams. Referring to **Fig. 3**, draw a diagonal line from corner to corner. Stitch ¼" on both sides of drawn line. Cut on drawn line to make 2 **small triangle units**. Repeat with remaining **small triangle-squares** to make a total of 4 **small triangle units**.

Fig. 2   **Fig. 3**

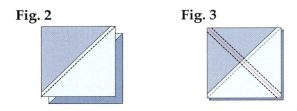

small triangle unit (make 4)

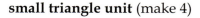

3. (*Note:* To prevent the Small Ohio Star from "floating" in the center of the Large Ohio Star, use a scant ¼" seam allowance when assembling.) Sew **very small squares**, **small triangle units**, and **center square** together to make **Small Ohio Star**.

Small Ohio Star (make 1)

4. Use very light blue and medium blue **large rectangles** and follow Step 1 to make 4 **large triangle-squares**, drawing squares 4⅜" x 4⅜".
5. Using **large triangle-squares**, repeat Step 2 to make 4 **large triangle units**.
6. Sew **medium squares**, **large triangle units**, and **Small Ohio Star** together to make **Large Ohio Star**.

Large Ohio Star (make 1)

7. To make triangle-square A's, place very light blue and light blue **large rectangles** right sides together. Referring to **Fig. 4**, follow **Making Triangle-Squares**, page 147, to make a total of 16 **triangle-square A's**.

Fig. 4

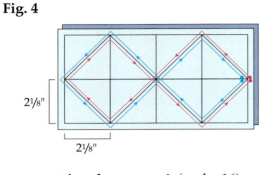

2⅛"

2⅛"

triangle-square A (make 16)

8. To make triangle-square B's, place very light blue and light blue **squares** right sides together. Referring to **Fig. 5**, follow **Making Triangle-Squares**, page 147, to make 32 **triangle-square B's**.

Fig. 5

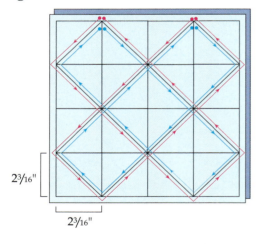

2³⁄₁₆"

2³⁄₁₆"

triangle-square B (make 32)

9. Sew 1 **triangle B** and 4 **triangle-square B's** together to make **Unit 1**. Make 4 **Unit 1's**. Sew 2 **triangle B's** and 4 **triangle-squares B's** together to make **Unit 2**. Make 4 **Unit 2's**.

Unit 1 (make 4)   Unit 2 (make 4)

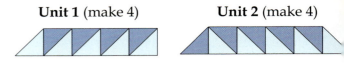

10. Sew 1 **large triangle** and 1 **Unit 1** together to make **Unit 3**, leaving portion of seam shown in pink unstitched at this time. Make 4 **Unit 3's**.

Unit 3 (make 4)

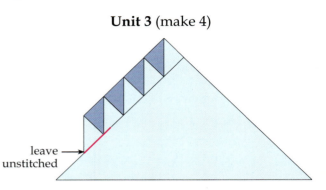

leave → unstitched

11. Sew 1 **Unit 2**, 1 **Unit 3**, and 2 **medium triangles** together to make **Unit 4**, leaving portion of seam shown in pink unstitched at this time. Make 4 **Unit 4's**.

Unit 4 (make 4)

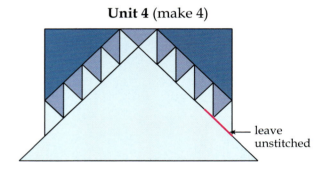

leave ← unstitched

12. Sew 1 **diamond**, 1 **triangle A**, and 2 **triangle-square A's** together to make **Unit 5**, matching "A" side of diamond with triangle A. Make 4 **Unit 5's**. Sew 1 reverse **diamond**, 1 **triangle A**, 2 **triangle-square A's**, and **1 small square** together to make **Unit 6**, matching "A" side of diamond with triangle A. Make 4 **Unit 6's**.

Unit 5 (make 4)   Unit 6 (make 4)

13. Sew 1 **Unit 5**, 1 **Unit 6**, and 1 **large square** together to make **Corner Block**. Make 4 **Corner Blocks**.

Corner Block (make 4)

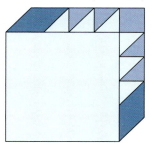

4. Sew **Corner Blocks**, **Unit 4's**, and **Large Ohio Star** together into rows (**Fig. 6**). Sew long seams to join rows, then finish sewing portions of seams left unsewn in Steps 10 and 11 to complete **Feathered Star**.

Fig. 6

5. Follow **Adding Mitered Borders**, page 151, to attach **inner border strips** to **Feathered Star** to complete **Inner Border**.

BORDER #1

. Place 1 **square** on 1 **rectangle** with right sides together and stitch diagonally as shown in **Fig. 7**. Trim 1/4" from stitching line as shown in **Fig. 8**. Press open, pressing seam allowance toward darker fabric.

Fig. 7   **Fig. 8**

2. Place 1 **square** on opposite end of **rectangle**. Stitch diagonally as shown in **Fig. 9**. Trim and press open as in Step 1 to complete **Wild Goose Unit**.

Fig. 9   **Wild Goose Unit** (make 80)

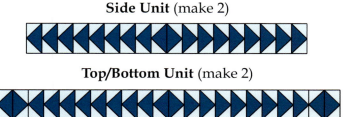

3. Repeat Steps 1 and 2 to make 80 **Wild Goose Units**.
4. Sew together 18 **Wild Goose Units** to make each **Side Unit** and 22 **Wild Goose Units** to make each **Top/Bottom Unit**.

Side Unit (make 2)

Top/Bottom Unit (make 2)

5. Sew **Side**, then **Top** and **Bottom Units** to **Inner Border**.
6. Follow **Adding Mitered Borders**, page 151, to attach **border #1 strips** to complete **Border #1**.

BORDER #2

1. To make triangle-squares, place 1 light blue print and 1 dark blue solid **rectangle** right sides together. Referring to **Fig. 10**, follow **Making Triangle-Squares**, page 147, to make 70 **triangle-squares**. Repeat with remaining rectangles to make a total of 140 **triangle-squares** (you will need 128 and have 12 left over).

Fig. 10

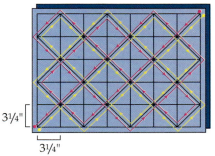

3¼"   3¼"

triangle-square (make 140)

2. Using **triangle-squares**, repeat Step 2, page 33, to make 128 **triangle units**.
3. Sew 4 **squares**, 4 **triangle units**, and 1 **center square** together to make **Ohio Star Block**. Make 32 **Ohio Star Blocks**.

Ohio Star Block (make 32)

4. Referring to **Quilt Top Diagram**, page 38, sew together 7 **Ohio Star Blocks** to make each **Side Unit** and 9 **Ohio Star Blocks** to make each **Top/Bottom Unit**. Sew **Side**, then **Top** and **Bottom Units** to **Border #1**.
5. Follow **Adding Mitered Borders**, page 151, to attach **border #2 strips** to complete **Border #2**.

BORDER #3 and OUTER BORDER

1. To make triangle-squares, place 1 very light blue and 1 medium blue **rectangle** right sides together. Referring to **Fig. 11**, follow **Making Triangle-Squares**, page 147, to make 84 **triangle-squares**. Repeat with remaining **rectangles** to make a total of 168 **triangle-squares** (you will need 144 and have 24 left over).

Fig. 11

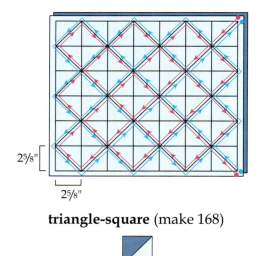

triangle-square (make 168)

2. Sew 1 **medium triangle**, 3 **triangle-squares**, and 1 **large triangle** together to make **Unit 7**. Make 20 **Unit 7's**.

Unit 7 (make 20)

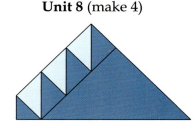

3. Sew 1 **small triangle**, 3 **triangle-squares**, and 1 **large triangle** together to make **Unit 8**. Make 4 **Unit 8's**.

Unit 8 (make 4)

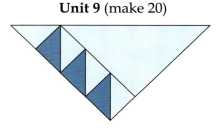

4. Sew 1 **medium triangle**, 3 **triangle-squares**, and 1 **large triangle** together to make **Unit 9**. Make 20 **Unit 9's**.

Unit 9 (make 20)

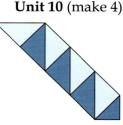

5. Sew 1 **medium triangle**, 3 **triangle-squares**, and 1 **small triangle** together to make **Unit 10**. Make 4 **Unit 10's**.

Unit 10 (make 4)

6. Sew 1 **Unit 8**, 5 **Unit 9's**, 5 **Unit 7's**, and 1 **Unit 10** together to make **Border Unit**. Make 4 **Border Units**.

Border Unit (make 4)

- Referring to **Quilt Top Diagram**, page 38, sew 1 **Border Unit** to each side of quilt top. Sew 1 **small triangle** into each corner. Sew **corner triangles** to corners.
- Follow **Adding Squared Borders**, page 150, to attach **side**, then **top** and **bottom border #3 strips** to complete **Border #3**.
- Follow **Adding Squared Borders** to attach **side**, then **top** and **bottom outer border strips** to complete **Quilt Top**.

COMPLETING THE QUILT
- Follow **Quilting**, page 151, to mark, layer, and quilt, using **Quilting Diagram**, page 39, as a suggestion. Our quilt is hand quilted.
- Cut a 32" square of binding fabric. Follow **Binding**, page 155, to bind quilt using 2¹⁄₂"w bias binding with mitered corners.

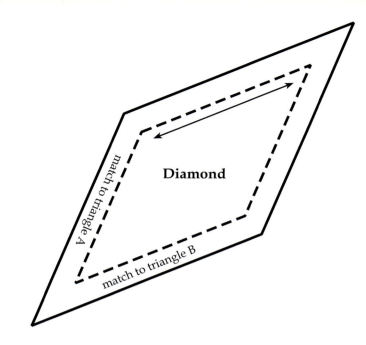

Diamond

match to triangle A

match to triangle B

Assembly Diagram

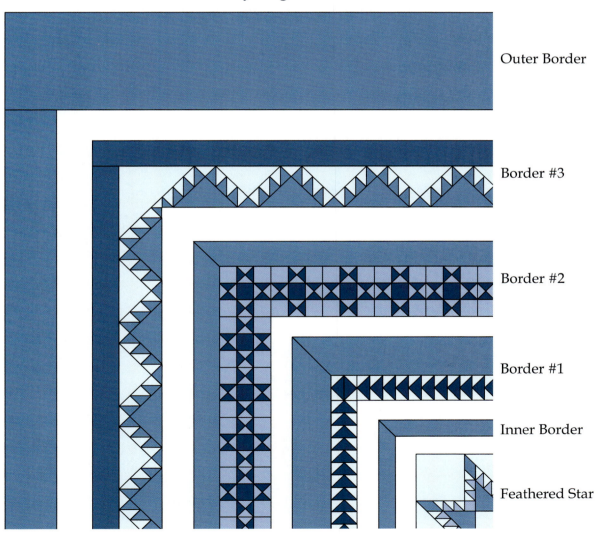

Outer Border

Border #3

Border #2

Border #1

Inner Border

Feathered Star

Quilt Top Diagram

Quilting Diagram

--- — — — **QUICK TIP** - — — — ---

ORGANIZING A COMPLEX PIECING PROJECT

A complex quilt like our O My Stars! Quilt, page 32, can be a little intimidating, but some pre-planning and careful organization can make a project of this size a much more manageable undertaking. The following suggestions may be helpful.

- *When instructions divide a quilt into sections, treat the sections as separate projects during the construction process. This will make organizing the entire project easier and will let you work on the different sections at different times, avoiding mistakes caused by mixing the pieces or confusing the instructions.*

- *Make notes on your instructions as cutting and construction steps are completed. This will be especially helpful when you return to work on a project that has been put away. If you prefer not to mark on your original instructions, use self-stick notes or attach notes with removable tape.*

- *Label **all** quilt pieces **as they are cut**. This is the most important step in preventing confusion later during the construction process. Use paper labels pinned to the pieces or place the groups of pieces into labeled resealable plastic bags. As you use the pieces, make sure remaining ones are re-labeled or returned to the proper bag.*

- *Use separate boxes or larger resealable plastic bags to hold all the groups of pieces for each separate section of the quilt throughout the construction process. Label these boxes or bags with the name of the section and include in them any special tools or materials needed, as well as notes pertaining to that section.*

- *Keep these smaller containers together in a larger box or basket in which you can also keep your instructions, extra yardage, thread, and other notions for the project.*

FEATHERED STAR WALL HANGING

SKILL LEVEL: 1 2 3 4 5
WALL HANGING SIZE: 43" x 43"

Our wall hanging repeats the center section of the O My Stars! quilt. Please refer to the Assembly Diagram for the quilt on page 37 for section names when selecting fabrics and while assembling the wall hanging top.

YARDAGE REQUIREMENTS

Yardage is based on 45"w fabric.

- ☐ 1³/₈ yds **total** of very light blue prints:
  ³/₄ yd for Feathered Star
  ⁵/₈ yd for Border #1
- ☐ ³/₈ yd of light blue print for Feathered Star
- ☐ ³/₄ yd **total** of medium blue prints:
  ³/₈ yd for Feathered Star
  ³/₈ yd for Inner Border
- ☐ ¹/₂ yd of dark blue solid for Border #1
  2⁷/₈ yds for backing and hanging sleeve
  ³/₄ yd for binding
  46" x 46" batting

MAKING THE WALL HANGING

1. Follow **Cutting Out the Pieces**, pages 32 - 33, to cut pieces indicated for **Feathered Star**, **Inner Border**, and **Border #1** only.
2. Follow **Assembling the Quilt Top** through **Border #1**, pages 33 - 35, to make **Wall Hanging Top**.
3. Follow **Quilting**, page 151, to mark, layer, and quilt, using **Quilting Diagram**, page 39, as a suggestion. Our wall hanging is hand quilted.
4. Follow **Making a Hanging Sleeve**, page 157, to attach hanging sleeve to wall hanging.
5. Cut a 24" square of binding fabric. Follow **Binding**, page 155, to bind wall hanging using 2¹/₂"w bias binding with mitered corners.

OHIO STAR VALANCE

BLOCK SIZE: 9³/₈" x 9³/₈"
VALANCE SIZE: 12¹/₂" x 47"

Our valance will fit an approximately 36"w window.

YARDAGE REQUIREMENTS

Yardage is based on 45"w fabric.

- ☐ 1¹/₂ yds of dark blue print
- ☐ ³/₄ yd of light blue print
- ☐ ¹/₂ yd of medium blue print
  1¹/₂ yds for backing
  3⁵/₈ yds of 2¹/₄"w bias strip for welting
  3⁵/₈ yds of ⁵/₁₆" cord for welting
  1³/₈ yds of fusible fleece

CUTTING OUT THE PIECES

All measurements include a ¼" seam allowance. Follow Rotary Cutting, page 144, to cut fabric.

1. **From dark blue print:** ☐
   - Cut 2 lengthwise **border strips** 2¹/₄" x 47³/₈".

2. **From light blue print:** ☐
   - Cut 1 strip 1¹/₂"w. From this strip, cut 20 **very small squares** 1¹/₂" x 1¹/₂".
   - Cut 2 strips 3⁵/₈"w. From these strips, cut 20 **medium squares** 3⁵/₈" x 3⁵/₈".
   - Cut 1 **large rectangle** 15" x 19" for large triangle-squares.
   - Cut 1 **small rectangle** 8" x 10" for small triangle-squares.

3. **From medium blue print:** ☐
   - Cut 1 **large rectangle** 15" x 19" for large triangle-squares.
   - Cut 1 **small rectangle** 8" x 10" for small triangle-squares.
   - Cut 5 **center squares** 1¹/₂" x 1¹/₂".

ASSEMBLING THE VALANCE

Follow Piecing and Pressing, page 146, to make valance.

1. To make small triangle-squares, place **small rectangles** right sides together. Referring to **Fig. 1** follow **Making Triangle-Squares**, page 147, to make 24 **small triangle-squares** (you will need 20 and have 4 left over).

Fig. 1

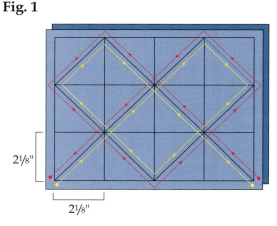

2¹/₈"

2¹/₈"

small triangle-square (make 24)

2. Follow Steps 2 and 3 of **Assembling the Quilt Top**, page 33, to make 5 **Small Ohio Stars**.
3. Using **large rectangles**, follow Step 1 to make 24 **large triangle-squares**, drawing squares 4³/₈" x 4³/₈".

- Follow Steps 5 and 6 of **Assembling the Quilt Top**, page 33, to make 5 **Large Ohio Stars**.
- Referring to photo, sew **Large Ohio Stars** into a row.
- Sew **border strips** to long edges of row to complete **Valance Top**.

COMPLETING THE VALANCE

- Follow Step 2 of **Adding Welting to Pillow Top**, page 158, to make welting. Cut welting into 2 equal lengths.
- Matching raw edges, baste welting to top and bottom edges of valance top, using a 1/2" seam allowance.
- Cut fusible fleece 1/2" smaller on all sides than valance top. Follow manufacturer's instructions to center and fuse fleece to wrong side of valance top.
- Cut valance back same size as valance top. Matching right sides and raw edges, pin and stitch valance top to back along top and bottom edges, stitching as close as possible to welting.
- Press ends of valance 1/4" to wrong side. Turn valance right side out. To form rod pockets, stitch along side, then top and bottom edges of row, leaving ends of border strips open (**Fig. 2**).

Fig. 2

WILD GOOSE TIEBACKS

SIZE: 3 1/2" x 25"

Instructions are for making 2 tiebacks.

YARDAGE REQUIREMENTS
Yardage is based on 45"w fabric.

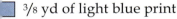 3/8 yd of light blue print
1/4 yd of medium blue print
3/8 yd for backing
3 1/2 yds of 2"w bias strip for welting
3 1/2 yds of 7/32" cord for welting
1/4 yd of fusible fleece

You will also need:
    4 small cabone (drapery) rings

CUTTING OUT THE PIECES
All measurements include a 1/4" seam allowance. Follow Rotary Cutting, page 144, to cut fabric.

1. **From light blue print:**
    - Cut 4 strips 2"w. From these strips, cut 64 **squares** 2" x 2".
2. **From medium blue print:**
    - Cut 2 strips 3 1/2"w. From these strips, cut 32 **rectangles** 2" x 3 1/2".

MAKING THE TIEBACKS
Follow Piecing and Pressing, page 146, to make tiebacks.

1. Using **rectangles** and **squares**, follow Steps 1 and 2 of **Border #1**, page 35, to make 32 **Wild Goose Units**.
2. Sew 16 **Wild Goose Units** together to make each tieback top.

Tieback Top (make 2)

3. Follow Step 2 of **Adding Welting to Pillow Top**, page 158, to make welting. Cut welting into 2 equal lengths.
4. Follow Steps 3 and 4 of **Adding Welting to Pillow Top** to baste welting to each tieback top.
5. Cut back same size as each tieback top. Matching right sides and raw edges, pin and stitch each tieback top to back along all edges, stitching as close as possible to welting and leaving an opening for turning.
6. Cut fusible fleece 1/4" smaller on all sides than each tieback top. Follow manufacturer's instructions to center and fuse fleece to wrong side of each tieback top.
7. Turn right side out, turning corners completely; press. Blindstitch opening closed to complete each tieback.
8. Sew 1 ring to back at each end of tiebacks.

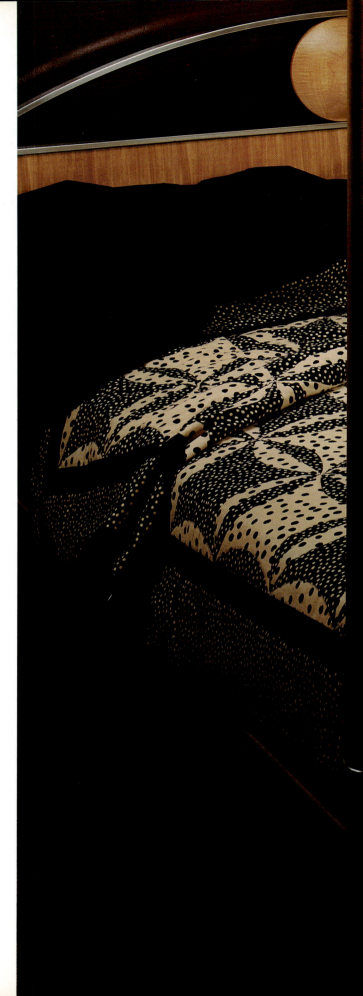

ROBBING PETER TO PAY PAUL

The name Robbing Peter to Pay Paul is a classic Quaker term that has been given to many different quilt patterns throughout the years. Depending on the region in which it was created, our contemporary version might also be called Dolley Madison's Workbox, Steeplechase, or Butter and Eggs. Although our design is very traditional, modern techniques save time and effort when creating the circular-looking blocks. We used a template to cut arc shapes from strip sets and then simply fused the motifs over large, plain fabric squares — so there's no worrisome curved piecing! Machine stitching with clear nylon thread provides a quick finish to the appliqués. For added ease, we completed our project with fast machine quilting.

ROBBING PETER TO PAY PAUL QUILT

SKILL LEVEL: 1 2 3 4 5
BLOCK SIZE: 9" x 9"
QUILT SIZE: 87" x 96"

YARDAGE REQUIREMENTS

Yardage is based on 45"w fabric.

- ■ 6³/₈ yds of black print
- ☐ 4⁷/₈ yds of tan print
- ■ 2⁵/₈ yds of black solid
  8 yds for backing
  1 yd for binding
  120" x 120" batting

You will also need:
transparent monofilament thread for appliqué
12 yds of 17¹/₄"w paper-backed fusible web

CUTTING OUT THE PIECES

All measurements include a ¼" seam allowance. Follow
Rotary Cutting, *page 144, to cut fabric.*

1. **From black print:** ■
    - Cut 37 **strips** 2"w.
    - Cut 2 lengthwise strips 5¹/₂" x 80" for **top/bottom outer borders**.
    - Cut 2 lengthwise strips 5¹/₂" x 99" for **side outer borders**.
    - From remaining fabric, cut 36 **squares** 9¹/₂" x 9¹/₂".

2. **From tan print:** ☐
    - Cut 37 **strips** 2"w.
    - Cut 9 strips 9¹/₂"w. From these strips, cut 36 **squares** 9¹/₂" x 9¹/₂".

3. **From black solid:** ■
    - Cut 2 lengthwise strips 2¹/₄" x 89" for **side inner borders**.
    - Cut 2 lengthwise strips 2¹/₄" x 76" for **top/bottom inner borders**.

ASSEMBLING THE QUILT TOP

*Follow **Piecing and Pressing**, page 146, to make quilt top.*

1. Sew 8 **squares** together to make **Row**. Make 9 **Rows**.

Row (make 9)

2. Sew **Rows** together to make **Center Section** of quilt top.

Center Section

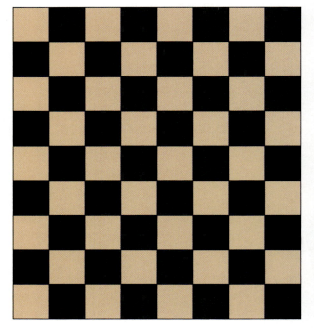

3. Sew **strips** together to make **Strip Set**. Make 32 **Strip Sets**.

Strip Set (make 32)

4. Follow manufacturer's instructions to fuse web to wrong sides of **Strip Sets** and remaining **strips**. Remove paper backing.

5. Follow Step 1 of **Template Cutting**, page 146, to make templates from patterns **A** and **B**, page 47.

6. Referring to Step 2 of **Template Cutting**, page 146 and placing center line of template on seamline, use **Template A** to cut 127 **A's** from **Strip Sets** (**Fig. 1**). Use **Template B** to cut 17 **B's** from remaining black print **strips** and 17 **B's** from remaining tan print **strips**.

Fig. 1

7. Referring to **Fig. 2**, follow Steps 4 - 14 of **Invisible Appliqué**, page 149, to stitch **A's** over seamlines of **Center Section** and to stitch **B's** at outside edges of outer squares.

Fig. 2

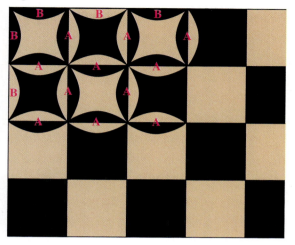

8. Follow **Adding Squared Borders**, page 150, to sew **top**, **bottom**, then **side inner borders** to **Center Section**. Add **top**, **bottom**, then **side outer borders** to complete **Quilt Top**.

COMPLETING THE QUILT

1. Follow **Quilting**, page 151, to mark, layer, and quilt, using **Quilting Diagram** as a suggestion. Our quilt is machine quilted.
2. Cut a 32" square of binding fabric. Follow **Binding**, page 155, to bind quilt using 2 1/2"w bias binding with mitered corners.

Quilting Diagram

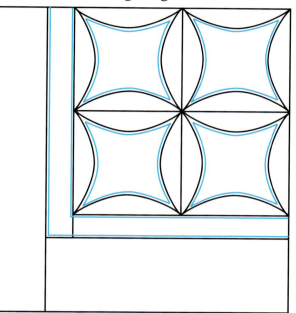

- - - - - - - - - **QUICK TIP** - - - - - - - - -

HANDLING A LARGE QUILT WHEN MACHINE QUILTING

The most difficult problems encountered when machine quilting often don't involve the actual quilting, but handling the bulk of a large quilt. You may want to try the following methods for managing the task.

- *Use a work surface large enough to accommodate the quilt. If necessary, use a folding table, an adjustable-height ironing board, or other portable table to extend your work surface to the left of and behind your sewing machine. The entire weight of the quilt must be supported to prevent it from pulling the area under the needle, which could cause distortion of your quilting stitches.*

- *When possible, keep the largest portion of the quilt to your left. Always begin quilting in the center and work toward the outside of the quilt to minimize the amount of quilt under the head of the sewing machine.*

- *Try different methods of holding the portion of the quilt that must pass under the head of the machine. Some quilters simply accordion-fold the quilt, letting it fan out behind the machine. Or, you may wish to roll up the quilt and use one of the many devices on the market for holding the roll in place. Round and oval bicycle clips or plastic clips made specifically for quilters are available. The rolled quilt may also be pinned with large safety pins.*

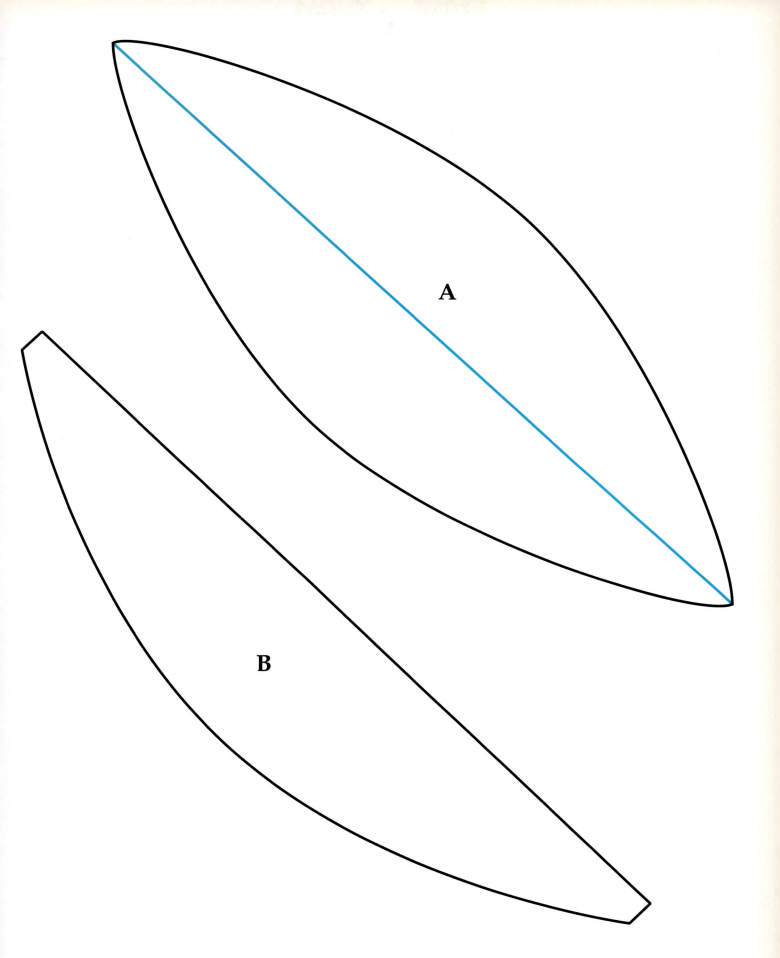

A

B

DRESDEN PLATE

During the Roaring '20's, Americans became enchanted by the delicate porcelain for which the Dresden region of Germany is known. But when the Great Depression came in the next decade, such luxuries were no longer affordable. However, inspired by the china's dainty scalloped edges and brilliant hues, quilters re-created that elegance through the Dresden Plate pattern, which became an instant classic. For our jewel-tone version, we developed a quick method to eliminate the raw edges of the "plates." We also used machine blindstitch, a faster way to achieve the look of hand appliqué.

DRESDEN PLATE QUILT

SKILL LEVEL: 1 2 3 4 5
BLOCK SIZE: 15½" x 15½"
QUILT SIZE: 90" x 109"

YARDAGE REQUIREMENTS

Yardage is based on 45"w fabric.

- ☐ 6¼ yds of cream solid
- 🟩 3 yds of green print
- 🟥 ¾ yd **each** of 2 pink prints, 2 red prints, 2 purple prints, and 1 dark green print
- 🟦 ⅝ yd of purple solid
- 2 yds of organdy or other very lightweight cotton fabric
- 8¼ yds for backing
- 1 yd for binding
- 120" x 120" batting

You will also need:
transparent monofilament thread for appliqué
pinking shears (optional)

CUTTING OUT THE PIECES

*All measurements include a ¼" seam allowance. Follow **Rotary Cutting**, page 144, and **Template Cutting**, page 146, to cut fabric.*

1. **From cream solid:**
   - Cut 2 lengthwise strips 6½" x 99" for **side borders**.
   - Cut 2 lengthwise strips 6½" x 94" for **top/bottom borders**.
   - Cut 7 strips 16"w. From these strips, cut 14 squares 16" x 16". From remaining fabric width, cut 6 squares 16" x 16" for a total of 20 **background squares**.

2. **From green print:** 🟩
   - Cut 5 strips 16"w. From these strips, cut 49 **sashing strips** 3½" x 16".
   - Cut 40 **A's** using **Template A** pattern, page 53.

3. **From *each* of the 2 pink prints, 2 red prints, 2 purple prints, and 1 dark green print:** 🟥
   - Cut 40 **A's** using **Template A**.

4. **From purple solid:** 🟦
   - Cut 3 strips 3½"w. From these strips, cut 30 **sashing squares** 3½" x 3½".
   - Cut 20 **B's** using **Template B** pattern, page 53.

5. **From organdy:**
   - Cut 32 strips 1½"w. From these strips, cut 320 **lining rectangles** 1½" x 4".
   - Cut 20 **B's** using **Template B**.

ASSEMBLING THE QUILT TOP

*Follow **Piecing and Pressing**, page 146, to make quilt top*

1. Referring to **Fig. 1**, place 1 **lining rectangle** and 1 **A** right sides together. Stitch from dot to dot ¼" from curved edge of **A**, backstitching at beginning and end of seam. Repeat with remaining **A's**.

Fig. 1

2. Referring to **Fig. 2**, trim excess lining fabric even with side edges of **A**; use pinking shears to trim seam allowance along curve to ⅛" (trim to ⅛" and clip curve if not using pinking shears). Repeat with remaining **A's**.

Fig. 2   **A** (make 320)

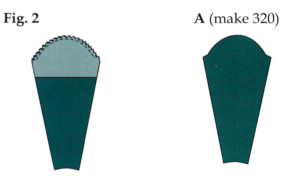

3. Referring to diagram for color placement, sew 16 **A's** together to make **Unit 1**. Make 20 **Unit 1's**.

Unit 1 (make 20)

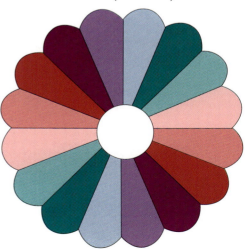

Place 1 purple **B** and 1 organdy **B** right sides together; stitch ¼" from edge. Use pinking shears to trim seam allowance to ⅛". To make opening for turning, cut a slit in organdy only (**Fig. 3**). Turn right side out and press. Repeat with remaining **B's**.

Fig. 3

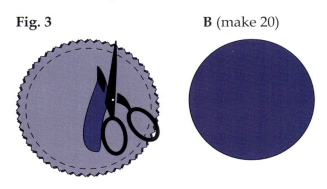

B (make 20)

Center 1 **B** over hole in center of 1 **Unit 1**. Follow **Mock Hand Appliqué**, page 149, to stitch **B** to **Unit 1** to make **Unit 2**. Make 20 **Unit 2's**.

Unit 2 (make 20)

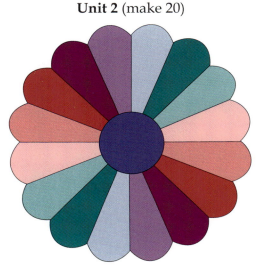

Fold **background square** in half twice and press folds; unfold. Using pressed lines as placement guidelines, center **Unit 2** on **background square**. Follow **Mock Hand Appliqué**, page 149, to stitch **Unit 2** to **background square** to complete **Block**. Make 20 **Blocks**.

Block (make 20)

7. Sew 5 **sashing strips** and 4 **Blocks** together to make **Row**. Make 5 **Rows**.

Row (make 5)

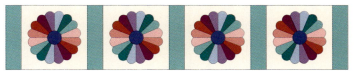

8. Sew 5 **sashing squares** and 4 **sashing strips** together to make **Sashing Row**. Make 6 **Sashing Rows**.

Sashing Row (make 6)

9. Referring to **Quilt Top Diagram**, page 52, sew **Sashing Rows** and **Rows** together to make center section of quilt top.
10. Follow **Adding Squared Borders**, page 150, to sew **side**, then **top** and **bottom borders** to center section to complete **Quilt Top**.

COMPLETING THE QUILT
1. Follow **Quilting**, page 151, to mark, layer, and quilt, using **Quilting Diagram**, page 53, as a suggestion. Our quilt is hand quilted using outline, feather, and cable designs.
2. Cut a 36" square of binding fabric. Follow **Binding**, page 155, to bind quilt using 2½"w bias binding with mitered corners.

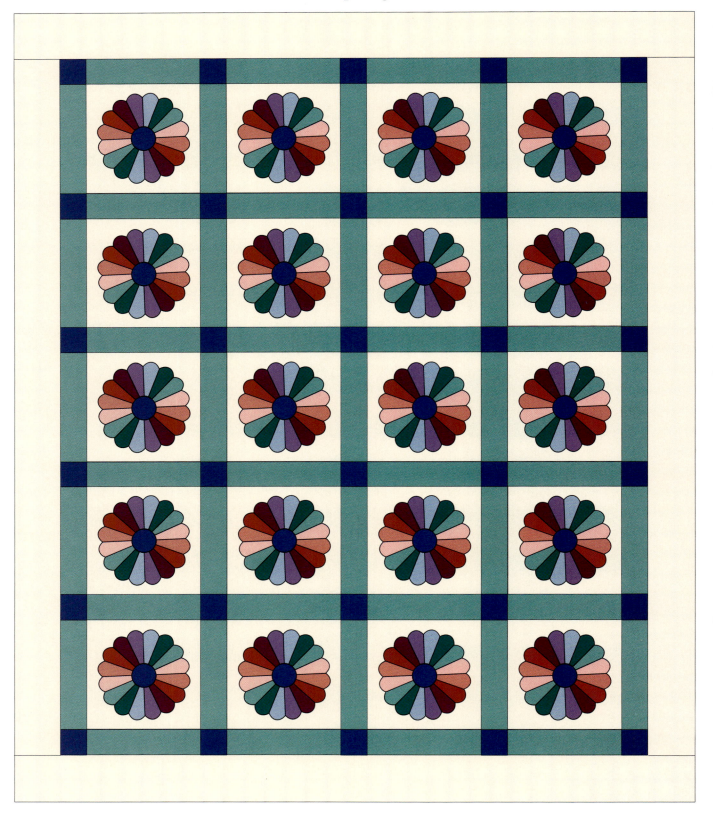

Quilting Diagram

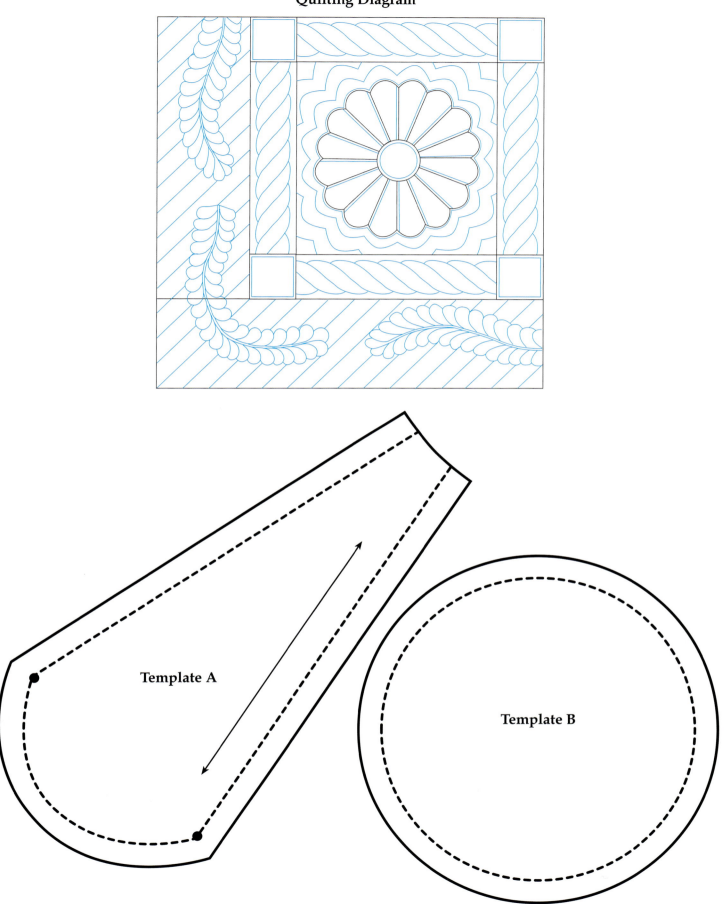

Template A

Template B

FLYING GEESE

One of autumn's most captivating images is the migration of majestic snow geese to their warm winter homes. Pioneer quilters were so awed by the sight that they captured those streamlined formations in the classic Flying Geese pattern. For our version of the design, we used a fast and extremely accurate paper foundation technique to create the triangle pieces. We simply "punched" the pattern onto sheets of tracing paper using an unthreaded sewing machine and then sewed the fabrics together on the paper foundations. With this updated method, it's simple to create perfectly pointed triangles every time! Easy to join together, the rows of "geese" are accented with solid sashing strips and a deep outer border.

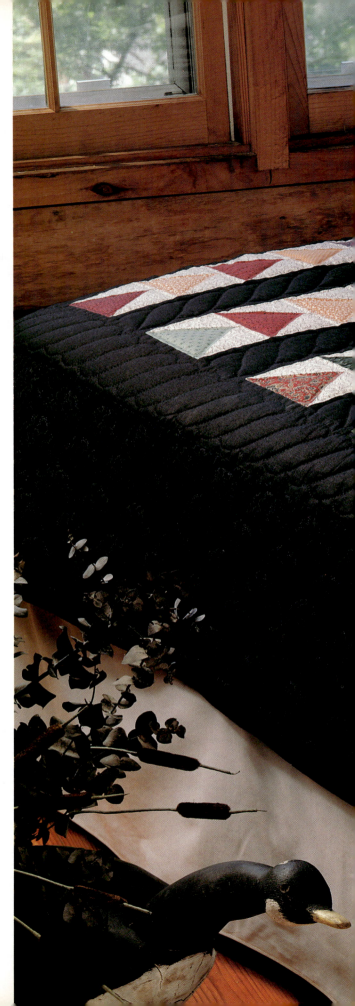

FLYING GEESE QUILT

SKILL LEVEL: 1 2 3 4 5
QUILT SIZE: 95" x 107"

YARDAGE REQUIREMENTS

Yardage is based on 45"w fabric. Due to the nature of paper foundation piecing, yardages given for light print and assorted dark prints are approximate.

- ■ 4³/₈ yds of black solid
- ▢ 5 yds of light print
- ◸ 4 yds **total** of assorted dark prints
- ■ 2⁵/₈ yds of black print
- ■ ¹/₂ yd of purple solid
  8⁵/₈ yds for backing
  1 yd for binding
  120" x 120" batting

You will also need:
    tracing paper

CUTTING OUT THE BORDERS AND SASHING

All measurements include a ¼" seam allowance. Follow **Rotary Cutting**, *page 144, to cut fabric.*

1. **From black solid:** ■
   - Cut 7 lengthwise strips 4¹/₄" x 78¹/₂" for **sashing strips**.
   - Cut 2 lengthwise strips 4¹/₄" x 78¹/₂" for **side inner borders**.
   - Cut 2 lengthwise strips 4¹/₄" x 66³/₄" for **top/bottom inner borders**.

2. **From black print:** ■
   - Cut 2 lengthwise strips 10¹/₂" x 86" for **side outer borders**.
   - Cut 2 lengthwise strips 10¹/₂" x 74¹/₄" for **top/bottom outer borders**.

3. **From purple solid:** ■
   - Cut 4 **inner border squares** 4¹/₄" x 4¹/₄".
   - Cut 4 **outer border squares** 10¹/₂" x 10¹/₂".

PIECING WITH PAPER FOUNDATIONS

1. Trace **Foundation Pattern**, page 59, onto 1 sheet of tracing paper. Do not cut out.
2. To make foundations, stack up to 12 sheets of tracing paper together and pin traced pattern on top, being careful not to pin over traced lines. Use an unthreaded sewing machine with stitch length set at approximately 8 stitches per inch to "sew" over traced lines of pattern, perforating the paper through all layers. Trim **foundations** to approximately ¹/₄" from outer line. Make a total of 64 **foundations**.

3. Fabric pieces for paper foundation piecing do not have to be cut precisely since they will be trimmed after stitching. To cut pieces for center triangles, "rough cut" a triangle from a dark print ³/₄" - 1" larger than Section 1 on the **foundation**. Triangle should be large enough to extend at least ¹/₄" past the section outline when placed right side up over Section 1. Cut 3 assorted **dark print pieces** to cover a triangle this size.
4. To cut pieces to cover triangles along left edge of foundations, repeat Step 3 to cut 3 **left edge pieces** from light print fabric using Section 2 on the **foundation** as a guide.
5. To cut pieces to cover triangles along right edge of foundations, repeat Step 3 to cut 3 **right edge pieces** from light print fabric using Section 3 on the **foundation** as a guide.
6. To secure first fabric piece to foundation, place 1 **dark print piece**, right side up, over Section 1 on **foundation**; pin in place (**Fig. 1**).

Fig. 1

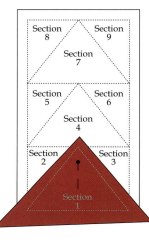

7. To sew left edge piece to foundation, place 1 **left edge piece** wrong side up on foundation so that edge of piece extends at least ¹/₄" past line between Sections 1 and 2 (**Fig. 2a**). Turn **foundation** over to paper side and sew pieces together directly on top of line between Sections 1 and 2, extending stitching a few stitches beyond beginning and end of line. Turn to fabric side and trim seam allowances to ¹/₄". Referring to **Fig. 2b**, open out **left edge piece**, press, and pin to **foundation**.

Fig. 2a   **Fig. 2b**

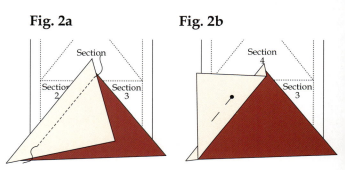

To sew right edge piece to foundation, place 1 **right edge piece** wrong side up on **foundation** so that edge of piece extends at least ¼" past line between Sections 1 and 3 (**Fig. 3a**). Turn **foundation** over to paper side and sew pieces together directly on top of line between Sections 1 and 3, extending stitching a few stitches beyond beginning and end of line. Turn to fabric side and trim seam allowances to ¼". Referring to **Fig. 3b**, open out **right edge piece**, press, and pin to **foundation**.

Fig. 3a   **Fig. 3b**

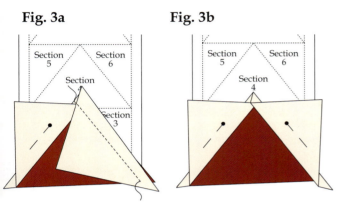

. Referring to **Foundation Pattern** for sewing sequence, continue sewing **dark print pieces**, **left edge pieces**, and **right edge pieces** to **foundation** until foundation is completely covered.

0. To complete **Flying Geese Unit**, trim fabric and foundation ¼" from outermost lines. Carefully tear away **foundation**.

Flying Geese Unit

1. Repeat Steps 3 - 10 to make a total of 64 **Flying Geese Units**.

ASSEMBLING THE QUILT TOP
Follow Pressing and Piecing, page 146, to make quilt top.

1. Sew 8 **Flying Geese Units** together to make **Flying Geese Strip**. Make 8 **Flying Geese Strips**.

Flying Geese Strip (make 8)

2. Referring to **Quilt Top Diagram**, page 58, sew **Flying Geese Strips** and **sashing strips** together to make center section of quilt top.
3. Sew 1 **inner border square** to each end of each **side inner border**. Sew **top**, **bottom**, then **side inner borders** to center section.
4. Sew 1 **outer border square** to each end of each **side outer border**. Sew **top**, **bottom**, then **side outer borders** to center section to complete **Quilt Top**.

COMPLETING THE QUILT
1. Follow **Quilting**, page 151, to mark, layer, and quilt, using **Quilting Diagram** as a suggestion. Our quilt is hand quilted using clamshell, cable, feather wreath, and heart designs.
2. Cut a 34" square of binding fabric. Follow **Binding**, page 155, to bind quilt using 2½"w bias binding with mitered corners.

Quilting Diagram

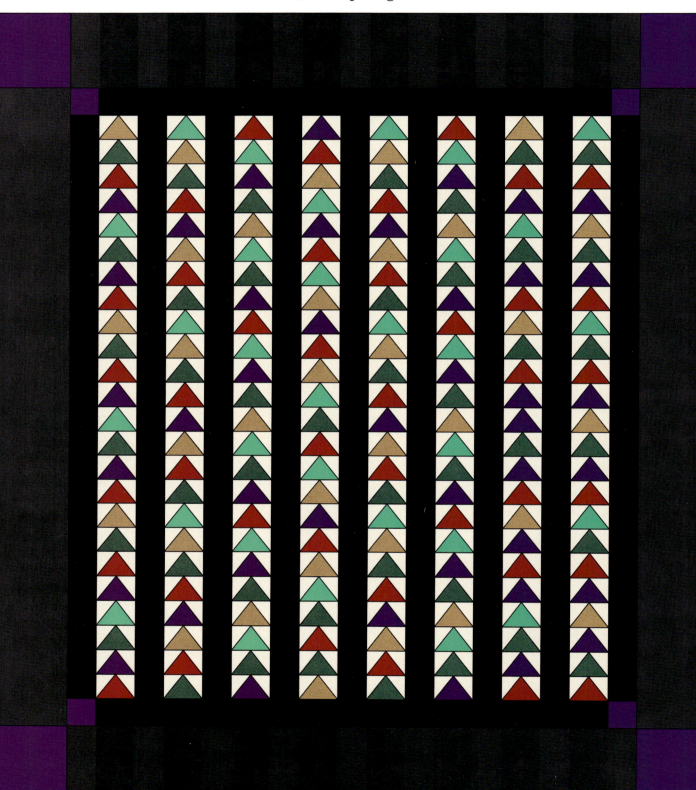

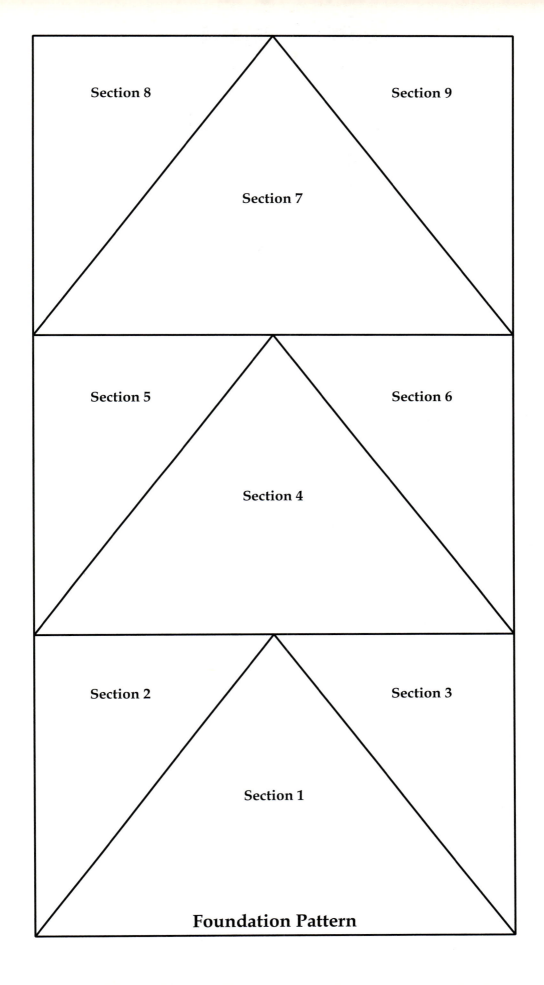

Section 8   Section 9

Section 7

Section 5   Section 6

Section 4

Section 2   Section 3

Section 1

Foundation Pattern

PASTEL POSIES COLLECTION

The field of delicate blossoms in our *Pastel Posies Collection will lull a little girl into blissful dreams! A combination of alternating patchwork and appliqué blocks, the pretty quilt features a simple flower motif that's fused in place and edged with machine stitching. And our fast technique for finishing the floral block will help you create accurate triangle corners without the worry of cutting angles! Complementing the appliqué design is the elementary Nine-Patch block, which we strip pieced using rotary-cut units. Basic grid and straight-line quilting provide a neat finishing touch.*

Our clever techniques make it easy to create an assortment of enchanting accessories in no time! A smaller version of our Pastel Posies quilt, the wall hanging (opposite) is even faster to sew. To create a charming bedside lamp (left), simply cover a lamp base with matching fabric and embellish the covered shade with fused-on motifs and trims. A bouquet of appliquéd posies blooms in the centers of our ruffled pillow shams (below).

PASTEL POSIES QUILT

SKILL LEVEL: 1 2 3 4 5
BLOCK SIZE: 8" x 8"
QUILT SIZE: 89" x 97"

YARDAGE REQUIREMENTS

Yardage is based on 45"w fabric.

- 5⁷/₈ yds of white print
- 4¹/₂ yds of floral print
- 2⁷/₈ yds of green solid
- 2⁵/₈ yds of pink print
- ⁵/₈ yd of light pink solid
  8¹/₈ yds for backing
  1 yd for binding
  120" x 120" batting

You will also need:
  paper-backed fusible web
  transparent monofilament thread for appliqué

CUTTING OUT THE PIECES

All measurements include a ¼" seam allowance. Follow Rotary Cutting, page 144, to cut fabric.

1. **From white print:**
   - Cut 20 **wide strips** 3¹/₂"w.
   - Cut 14 strips 9"w. From these strips, cut 55 **large squares** 9" x 9".

2. **From floral print:**
   - Cut 10 **narrow strips** 2¹/₂"w.
   - Cut 8 **wide strips** 3¹/₂"w.
   - Cut 2 lengthwise strips 3¹/₂" x 94" for **side outer borders**.
   - Cut 2 lengthwise strips 3¹/₂" x 92" for **top/bottom outer borders**.

3. **From green solid:**
   - Cut 2 lengthwise strips 1¹/₄" x 92" for **side inner borders**.
   - Cut 2 lengthwise strips 1¹/₄" x 86" for **top/bottom inner borders**.

4. **From pink print:**
   - Cut 19 strips 3¹/₂"w. From these strips, cut 220 **medium squares** 3¹/₂" x 3¹/₂".
   - Cut 4 **narrow strips** 2¹/₂"w.

PREPARING THE APPLIQUÉS

Use patterns, page 66, and follow Steps 1 - 3 of Invisible Appliqué, page 148, to cut appliqués.

1. **From light pink solid:**
   - Cut 55 **Large Circles**.

2. **From pink print:**
   - Cut 55 **Small Circles**.

3. **From green solid:**
   - Cut 55 **Leaves**.
   - Cut 55 **Stems**.

64

ASSEMBLING THE QUILT TOP

Follow Piecing and Pressing, page 146, to make quilt top.

1. Referring to **Fig. 1**, follow Steps 4 - 14 of **Invisible Appliqué**, page 149, to stitch appliqués to centers of **large squares**. Trim each **large square** to 8¹/₂" x 8¹/₂".

   Fig. 1

2. Place 1 **medium square** on each corner of 1 **large square** with right sides together and stitch diagonally as shown in **Fig. 2**. Trim ¼" from stitching lines as shown in **Fig. 3**. Press open, pressing seam allowances toward darker fabric to make **Block A**. Make 55 **Block A's**.

   Fig. 2

   Fig. 3

   Block A (make 55)

Sew 2 **wide strips** and 1 **narrow strip** together to make **Strip Set A**. Make 10 **Strip Set A's**. Cut across **Strip Set A's** at 3½" intervals to make 110 **Unit 1's**.

Strip Set A (make 10)   **Unit 1** (make 110)

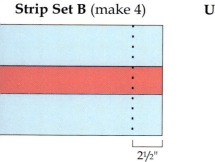
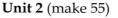
3½"

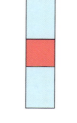

Sew 2 **wide strips** and 1 **narrow strip** together to make **Strip Set B**. Make 4 **Strip Set B's**. Cut across **Strip Set B's** at 2½" intervals to make 55 **Unit 2's**.

Strip Set B (make 4)   **Unit 2** (make 55)

2½"

Sew 2 **Unit 1's** and 1 **Unit 2** together to make **Block B**. Make 55 **Block B's**.

Block B (make 55)

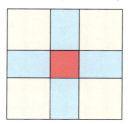

Sew 5 **Block A's** and 5 **Block B's** together to make **Row A**. Make 6 **Row A's**.

Row A (make 6)

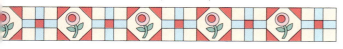

7. Sew 5 **Block B's** and 5 **Block A's** together to make **Row B**. Make 5 **Row B's**.

Row B (make 5)

8. Referring to **Quilt Top Diagram**, page 66, sew **Row A's** and **Row B's** together to make center section of quilt top.
9. Follow **Adding Squared Borders**, page 150, to sew **side**, then **top** and **bottom inner borders** to center section. Add **side**, then **top** and **bottom outer borders** to complete **Quilt Top**.

COMPLETING THE QUILT TOP
1. Follow **Quilting**, page 151, to mark, layer, and quilt, using **Quilting Diagram** as a suggestion. Our quilt is hand quilted.
2. Cut a 32" square of binding fabric. Follow **Binding**, page 155, to bind quilt using 2½"w bias binding with mitered corners.

Quilting Diagram

Quilt Top Diagram

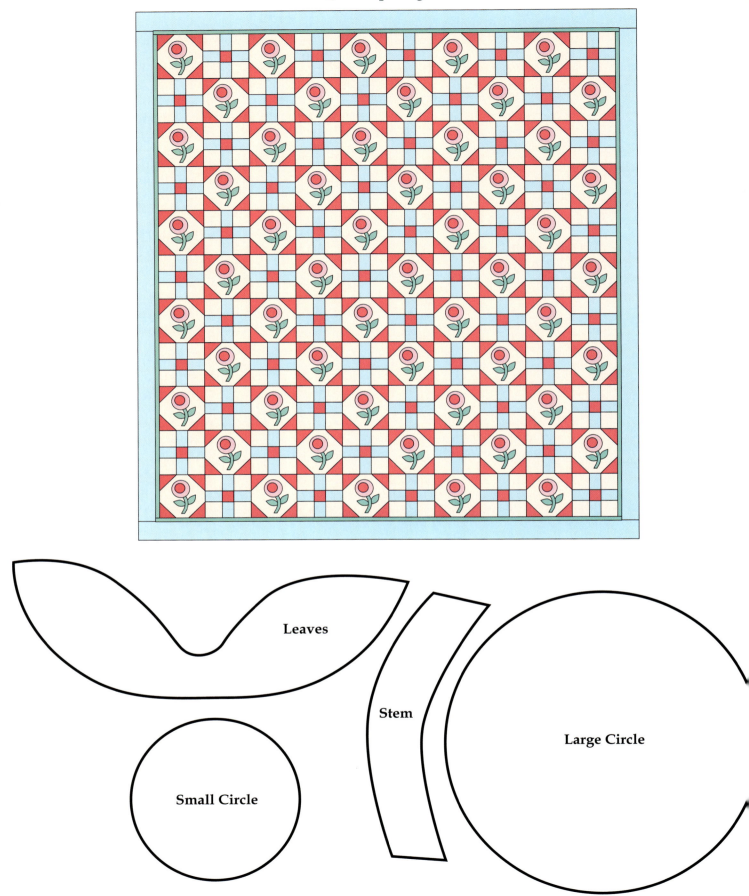

Leaves

Stem

Small Circle

Large Circle

POSY WALL HANGING

SKILL LEVEL: 1 **2** 3 4 5
BLOCK SIZE: 8" x 8"
WALL HANGING SIZE: 33" x 33"

YARDAGE REQUIREMENTS

Yardage is based on 45"w fabric.

- ☐ 7/8 yd of white print
- ☐ 5/8 yd of floral print
- ☐ 3/8 yd of pink print
- ☐ 1/4 yd of green solid
- ☐ 1/8 yd of light pink solid
- 1 1/8 yds for backing and hanging sleeve
- 5/8 yd for binding
- 35" x 35" batting

You will also need:
- paper-backed fusible web
- transparent monofilament thread for appliqué

CUTTING OUT THE PIECES

All measurements include a 1/4" seam allowance. Follow Rotary Cutting, page 144, to cut fabric.

From white print: ☐
- Cut 2 **wide strips** 3 1/2" x 21".
- Cut 2 strips 9"w. From these strips, cut 5 **large squares** 9" x 9".

From floral print: ☐
- Cut 2 **top/bottom outer borders** 3 1/2" x 32".
- Cut 2 **side outer borders** 3 1/2" x 26".
- Cut 1 **narrow strip** 2 1/2" x 21".
- Cut 2 **wide strips** 3 1/2" x 21".

From pink print: ☐
- Cut 2 strips 3 1/2"w. From these strips, cut 20 **medium squares** 3 1/2" x 3 1/2".
- Cut 1 **narrow strip** 2 1/2" x 21".

From green solid: ☐
- Cut 2 **top/bottom inner borders** 1 1/4" x 26".
- Cut 2 strips 1 1/4" x 24 1/2" for **side inner borders**.

PREPARING THE APPLIQUÉS

Use patterns, page 66, and follow Steps 1 - 3 of Invisible Appliqué, page 148, to cut appliqués.

From light pink solid: ☐
- Cut 5 **Large Circles**.

From pink print: ☐
- Cut 5 **Small Circles**.

From green solid: ☐
- Cut 5 **Leaves**.
- Cut 5 **Stems**.

ASSEMBLING THE WALL HANGING TOP

Follow Piecing and Pressing, page 146, to make wall hanging top.

1. Follow Steps 1 - 5 of **Assembling the Quilt Top** for **Pastel Posies Quilt**, page 64, to make 5 **Block A's** and 4 **Block B's** (you will need 8 **Unit 1's** cut from 1 **Strip Set A** and 4 **Unit 2's** cut from 1 **Strip Set B** for **Block B's**).

Block A (make 5)   **Block B** (make 4)

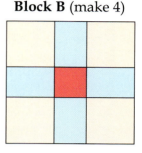

2. Referring to **Wall Hanging Top Diagram**, sew **Block A's** and **Block B's** together to make center section of wall hanging top.
3. Sew **side**, then **top** and **bottom inner borders** to center section. Add **side**, then **top** and **bottom outer borders** to complete **Wall Hanging Top**.

COMPLETING THE WALL HANGING

1. Follow **Quilting**, page 151, to mark, layer, and quilt, using **Quilting Diagram**, page 65, as a suggestion. Our wall hanging is hand quilted.
2. Follow **Making a Hanging Sleeve**, page 157, to attach hanging sleeve to wall hanging.
3. Cut a 21" square of binding fabric. Follow **Binding**, page 155, to bind wall hanging using 2 1/2"w bias binding with mitered corners.

Wall Hanging Top Diagram

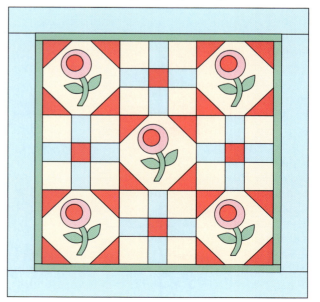

PASTEL PILLOW SHAMS

PILLOW SHAM SIZE: 22" x 26" (without ruffle)

Instructions are for making 2 pillow shams.

YARDAGE REQUIREMENTS

Yardage is based on 45"w fabric.

- ▢ 2¹⁄₈ yds of floral print
- ▢ ½ yd of white print
- ▢ ³⁄₈ yd of green solid
- ▢ ⅛ yd of light pink solid
- ▣ ⅛ yd of pink print
  2¼ yds for ruffle
  1⁵⁄₈ yds for sham top backings
  5½ yds of 3"w bias strip for welting
  5½ yds of ⁷⁄₃₂" cord for welting

You will also need:
  paper-backed fusible web
  transparent monofilament thread for appliqué

CUTTING OUT THE PIECES

*Follow **Rotary Cutting**, page 144, to cut fabric.*

1. **From floral print:** ▢
   - Cut 4 rectangles 16½" x 22½" for **sham backs**.
   - Cut 4 **side outer borders** 3³⁄₄" x 22½".
   - Cut 4 **top/bottom outer borders** 3³⁄₄" x 20½".

2. **From white print:** ▢
   - Cut 2 rectangles 15" x 20" for **sham tops**.

3. **From green solid:** ▣
   - Cut 4 strips 1¼"w. From **each** strip, cut 1 **top/bottom inner border** 1¼" x 19" and 1 **side inner border** 1¼" x 16".

MAKING THE SHAMS

1. Use patterns, page 66, and follow Steps 1 - 3 of **Invisible Appliqué**, page 148, to cut 10 **Stems** and 10 **Leaves** from green solid, 10 **Large Circles** from light pink solid, and 12 **Small Circles** from pink print.

2. Referring to **Sham Top Diagram**, follow Steps 4 - 14 of **Invisible Appliqué**, page 149, to stitch appliqués to each **sham top**. Trim **sham tops** to 14½" x 19".

3. Follow **Piecing and Pressing**, page 146, to sew **top**, **bottom**, then **side inner borders** to each **sham top**. Add **top**, **bottom**, then **side outer borders** to complete **Sham Tops**.

4. Follow **Quilting**, page 151, to mark, layer, and quilt. Our **Sham Tops** are hand quilted in the ditch around appliqués, with a diagonal grid on the background and inner borders, and with 2 outlines 1" apart on center of outer border.

5. Using a ½" seam allowance, follow **Adding Welting to Pillow Top**, page 158, and **Adding Ruffle to Pillow Top**, page 158, to add welting and a 3"w ruffle to each sham top.

6. On each **sham back** piece, press one 22½" edge ½" to the wrong side; press ½" to the wrong side again and stitch in place.

7. For each **Sham Back**, place 2 **sham back** pieces right side up. Referring to **Fig. 1**, overlap finished edges and baste in place.

Fig. 1

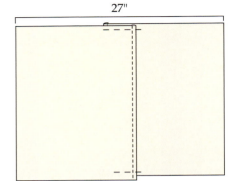

27"

8. To complete each sham, place **Sham Back** and **Sham Top** right sides together. Stitch through all layers as close as possible to welting. Cut corners diagonally; remove basting threads at opening. Turn **Sham** right side out; press.

Sham Top Diagram

BEDSIDE LAMP

SUPPLIES
  lamp with shade
  fabric to cover lamp base and shade
  fabric for shade trim
  satin ribbons for bow
  12" of ¼"w elastic
  paper-backed fusible web
  polyester fiberfill
  removable tape
  fabric glue
  spray adhesive
  tissue paper

COVERING THE LAMP AND LAMPSHADE

1. To cover lamp base, refer to **Fig. 1** to measure lamp from 1 side of neck to opposite side of neck; add 10".

Fig. 1

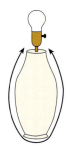

Cut a fabric square 2" larger than the measurement determined in Step 1. Fold fabric square in half from top to bottom and again from left to right.

To mark cutting line, tie 1 end of a piece of string to fabric marking pen. Insert a pin through string at ½ the measurement determined in Step 1. Insert pin through fabric as shown in **Fig. 2** and mark ¼ of a circle. Cut along drawn line through all layers of fabric. Unfold circle.

Fig. 2

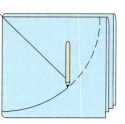

Center lamp on wrong side of fabric circle. Cut a small slit in fabric where lamp cord extends from base of lamp and pull cord through slit.

Bring edges of fabric up loosely around neck of lamp. Place fiberfill between lamp and fabric to achieve desired fullness. Gather fabric around neck and knot elastic securely around fabric and neck (**Fig. 3**). Fold edges of fabric to wrong side and tuck under elastic.

Fig. 3

6. Tie ribbons together into a bow around fabric, covering elastic.
7. To make pattern for covering lampshade, find seamline of shade. With tissue paper extending to right of shade seamline, match 1 edge of paper to seamline; use removable tape to tape in place. Allowing paper to overlap at seamline, wrap paper snugly around shade; tape in place (**Fig. 4**).

Fig. 4

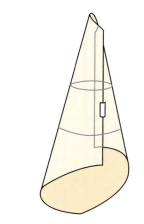

8. Mark along top and bottom edges of shade on paper. For overlap at seamline, draw a line on paper from top edge to bottom edge of shade 1" to the right of seamline. Remove paper from shade and cut out pattern along drawn lines.
9. Use pattern to cut shape from fabric.
10. Press 1 straight edge of fabric shape ½" to wrong side.
11. Using patterns on this page, follow Steps 1 - 3 of **Invisible Appliqué**, page 148, to fuse appliqués to fabric shape.
12. Matching unpressed straight edge of fabric shape to shade seamline, use spray adhesive to glue fabric to shade. Use fabric glue to glue pressed edge in place.
13. For trim, measure around top edge of shade; add 1". Cut a 1"w bias strip the determined measurement. Press each long edge and 1 end of fabric strip ¼" to wrong side. Beginning with unpressed end at seam of shade, glue strip along top edge of shade. Repeat for bottom edge of shade.

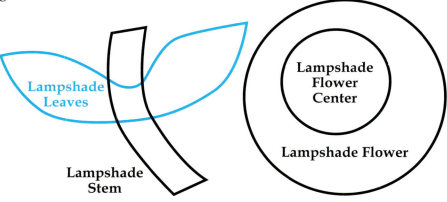

Lampshade Leaves

Lampshade Flower Center

Lampshade Flower

Lampshade Stem

COLORADO LOG CABIN

Developed in the mid-1800's, Elias Howe's sewing machine freed many seamstresses from tedious, time-consuming handwork. Quilters were quick to join the revolution, and the popular Log Cabin pattern became one of the first machine-pieced quilt designs. Along with a few of today's newest tools, machine stitching makes our dramatic Colorado Log Cabin a joy to create! After each "log" is stitched around the center square, it's rotary cut to an exact fit — so there are no tiny pieces to handle! And we make it easy to work in the LeMoyne Stars as you go, using a special angle-cutting ruler. The placement of the blocks and the deep border provide ample space for elegant quilting.

COLORADO LOG CABIN QUILT

SKILL LEVEL: 1 2 3 4 5
BLOCK SIZE: 12³/₈" x 12³/₈"
QUILT SIZE: 93" x 113"

YARDAGE REQUIREMENTS
Yardage is based on 45"w fabric.

 4¹/₄ yds **total** of assorted dark prints
4¹/₈ yds of cream solid
3¹/₄ yds of green solid
3¹/₄ yds of green print
1¹/₈ yds of red solid
8¹/₂ yds for backing
1 yd for binding
120" x 120" batting

You will also need:
    Companion Angle™ Rotary Cutting Ruler (made
      by EZ International)

CUTTING OUT THE PIECES
All measurements include a ¼" seam allowance. Follow
Rotary Cutting, *page 144, to cut fabric.*

1. **From assorted dark prints:**
    • Cut a total of 71 **strips** 1⁷/₈"w.

2. **From cream solid:**
    • Cut 68 **strips** 1⁷/₈"w.

3. **From green solid:**
    • Cut 2 lengthwise strips 3" x 103" for **side inner borders**.
    • From remaining fabric, cut 18 crosswise **strips** 1⁷/₈"w.

4. **From green print:**
    • Cut 2 lengthwise strips 7" x 103" for **side outer borders**.
    • Cut 2 lengthwise strips 7" x 96" for **top/bottom outer borders**.

5. **From red solid:**
    • Cut 14 **strips** 1⁷/₈"w.
    • Cut 3 strips 1⁷/₈"w. From these strips, cut 48 **squares** 1⁷/₈" x 1⁷/₈".

ASSEMBLING THE QUILT TOP
*Follow **Piecing and Pressing**, page 146, to make quilt top.*

1. Referring to **Fig. 1**, line up 45° marking (shown in pink) on rotary cutting ruler with lower edge of 1 red solid **strip**. Cut along right side of ruler to cut 1 end of **strip** at a 45° angle.

Fig. 1

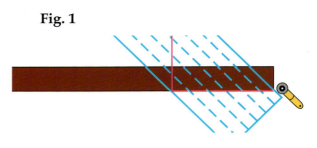

2. Turn cut **strip** 180° on mat and line up 45° marking on ruler with lower edge of **strip**. Line up previously cut 45° edge with 1⁷/₈" marking on the ruler. Cut **strip** at 1⁷/₈" intervals as shown in **Fig. 2** to cut **diamonds**.

Fig. 2

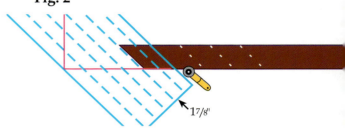

3. Repeat Steps 1 and 2 with remaining red and green solid **strips** to cut a total of 192 **red diamonds** and 192 **green diamonds**.

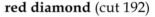

red diamond (cut 192)   **green diamond** (cut 192)

4. Line up 9" sewing line (dashed line) on Companion Angle ruler (4³/₄" from top of ruler) with bottom edge of of 1 dark print **strip**. Cut on both sides of ruler to make **trapezoid** (**Fig. 3**).

Fig. 3

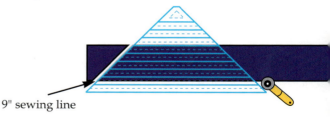

9" sewing line

5. Turn ruler 180° and line up ruler along same line with top edge of strip to cut another **trapezoid** (**Fig. 4**). Turning ruler after each cut, cut 96 **dark trapezoids** and 96 **light trapezoids** from remaining dark print and cream strips.

Fig. 4

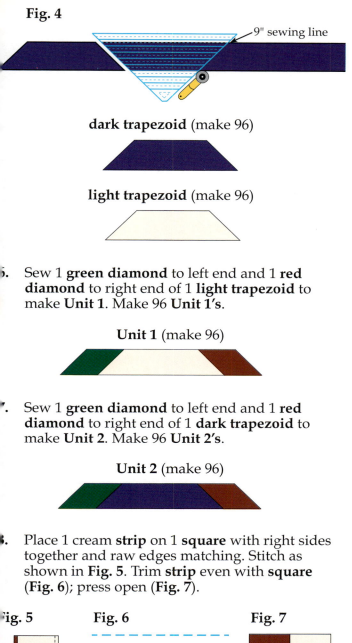

9" sewing line

dark trapezoid (make 96)

light trapezoid (make 96)

6. Sew 1 **green diamond** to left end and 1 **red diamond** to right end of 1 **light trapezoid** to make **Unit 1**. Make 96 **Unit 1's**.

Unit 1 (make 96)

7. Sew 1 **green diamond** to left end and 1 **red diamond** to right end of 1 **dark trapezoid** to make **Unit 2**. Make 96 **Unit 2's**.

Unit 2 (make 96)

8. Place 1 cream **strip** on 1 **square** with right sides together and raw edges matching. Stitch as shown in **Fig. 5**. Trim **strip** even with **square** (**Fig. 6**); press open (**Fig. 7**).

Fig. 5   **Fig. 6**   **Fig. 7**

9. Turn **square** ¼ turn to the left and repeat Step 8 to add the next "log" as shown in **Figs. 8 - 10**.

Fig. 8   **Fig. 9**   **Fig. 10**

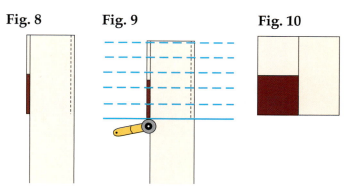

10. Repeat Step 9, adding 2 different dark **strips** to remaining 2 sides of **square** (**Fig. 11**).

Fig. 11

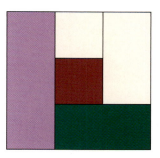

11. Continue adding **strips**, alternating 2 cream **strips** and 2 dark **strips** until there are 3 **strips** on each side of **square** to make **Unit 3**.

Unit 3 (make 48)

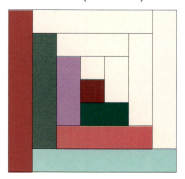

12. Repeat Steps 8 - 11 to make 48 **Unit 3's**.

13. (*Note:* Follow Steps 13 - 15 to make 48 **Blocks**.) Starting and stopping stitching exactly ¼" from edges of **Unit 3** and backstitching at each end, sew 1 **Unit 1** to 1 **Unit 3** (**Fig. 12**).

Fig. 12

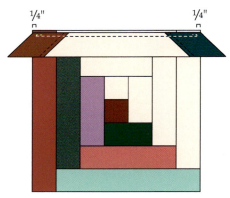

14. Repeat Step 13 to sew another **Unit 1**, then 2 **Unit 2's** to **Unit 3**, matching **light trapezoids** to light logs and **dark trapezoids** to dark logs.

15. To complete stitching at corners, fold 2 adjacent diamonds right sides together and stitch from end of previous stitching to outside edge, backstitching at beginning (**Fig. 13**). Repeat for remaining corners to complete **Block**.

Fig. 13

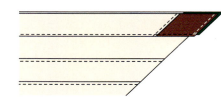

Block (make 48)

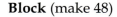

16. Sew 6 **Blocks** together to make **Row A**. Make 4 **Row A's**.

Row A (make 4)

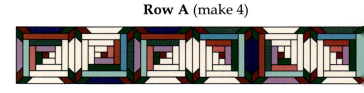

17. Sew 6 **Blocks** together to make **Row B**. Make 4 **Row B's**.

Row B (make 4)

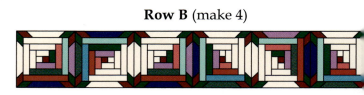

18. Referring to **Quilt Top Diagram**, sew **Rows** together to make center section of quilt top.

19. Follow **Adding Squared Borders**, page 150, to sew **side inner borders** to center section. Repeat to add **outer borders** to complete **Quilt Top**.

COMPLETING THE QUILT

1. Follow **Quilting**, page 151, to mark, layer, and quilt, using **Quilting Diagram** as a suggestion. Our quilt is hand quilted using cable and feather designs.

2. Cut a 34" square of binding fabric. Follow **Binding**, page 155, to bind quilt using 2½"w bias binding with mitered corners.

Quilting Diagram

OLD MAID'S PUZZLE

The designer of this Old Maid's Puzzle quilt may have used Hour Glass setting squares to jokingly suggest that time was running out for an unwed daughter. Also known as Double X and Kindergarten Block, the pattern is really child's play to stitch! You'll love the uncomplicated design, which is actually a variation of the basic Nine Patch. We used a simple grid-piecing method to create the triangle-squares and set the blocks with large sashing strips that are a breeze to assemble! Offering a complementary finish are the Dogtooth border and basic grid quilting.

OLD MAID'S PUZZLE QUILT

SKILL LEVEL: 1 2 3 4 5
BLOCK SIZE: 9" x 9"
QUILT SIZE: 82" x 91"

YARDAGE REQUIREMENTS

Yardage is based on 45"w fabric.

☐ 7⅞ yds of white solid

■ 3¼ yds of blue print
7½ yds for backing
1 yd for binding
90" x 108" batting

CUTTING OUT THE PIECES

*All measurements include a ¼" seam allowance. Follow
Rotary Cutting, page 144, to cut fabric.*

1. **From white solid:** ☐
   - Cut 18 strips 4¾"w. From these strips, cut 72
     sashing strips 4¾" x 9½".
   - Cut 9 strips 3½"w. From these strips, cut 108
     small squares 3½" x 3½".
   - Cut 10 strips 2"w. From these strips, cut 116
     small rectangles 2" x 3½".
   - Cut 2 **large squares** 18" x 18" for large
     triangle-squares.
   - Cut 2 lengthwise strips 1⅞" x 87½" for **side
     inner borders**.
   - Cut 2 lengthwise strips 2⅛" x 75¾" for
     top/bottom inner borders.
   - From remaining fabric, cut 9 **large rectangles**
     13" x 17" for small triangle-squares.

2. **From blue print:** ■
   - Cut 11 strips 2"w. From these strips, cut 232
     small squares 2" x 2".
   - Cut 9 **large rectangles** 13" x 17" for small
     triangle-squares.
   - Cut 2 **large squares** 18" x 18" for large
     triangle-squares.

ASSEMBLING THE QUILT TOP

*Follow Piecing and Pressing, page 146, to make
quilt top.*

1. To make small triangle-squares, place 1 blue and
   1 white **large rectangle** right sides together.
   Referring to **Fig. 1**, follow Steps 1 - 3 of **Making
   Triangle-Squares**, page 147, to draw a grid of 12
   squares 3⅞" x 3⅞". Referring to **Fig. 2** for
   stitching direction, follow Steps 4 - 6 of **Making
   Triangle-Squares** to make 24 **small triangle-
   squares**. Repeat with remaining **large rectangles**
   to make a total of 216 **small triangle-squares**.

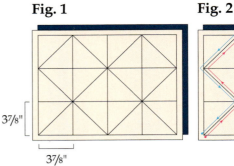

Fig. 1   **Fig. 2**

3⅞"

3⅞"

small triangle-square (make 216)

2. Sew 1 **small square** and 2 **small triangle-square**
   together to make **Unit 1**. Make 72 **Unit 1's**.

Unit 1 (make 72)

3. Sew 2 **small triangle-squares** and 1 **small squar**
   together to make **Unit 2**. Make 36 **Unit 2's**.

Unit 2 (make 36)

4. Sew 2 **Unit 1's** and 1 **Unit 2** together to make
   Block. Make 36 **Blocks**.

Block (make 36)

5. To make large triangle-squares, place 1 blue and
   1 white **large square** right sides together.
   Referring to **Fig. 3**, follow Steps 1 - 3 of **Making
   Triangle-Squares**, page 147, to draw a grid of 9
   squares 5½" x 5½". Referring to **Fig. 4** for
   stitching direction, follow Steps 4 - 6 of **Making
   Triangle-Squares** to make 18 **large triangle-
   squares**. Repeat with remaining **large squares** t
   make a total of 36 **large triangle-squares**.

Fig. 3   **Fig. 4**

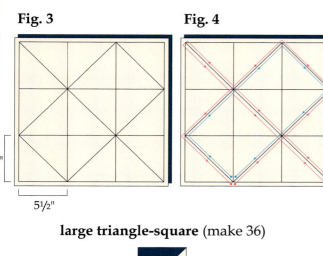

5½"

large triangle-square (make 36)

Place 2 **large triangle-squares** right sides and opposite colors together, matching seams (**Fig. 5**). Referring to **Fig. 6**, draw a diagonal line from corner to corner. Stitch ¼" on both sides of marked line. Cut on marked line and press open to make 2 **Sashing Blocks**. Repeat with remaining **large triangle-squares** to make a total of 36 **Sashing Blocks** (you will need 35 and have 1 left over).

Fig. 5   **Fig. 6**

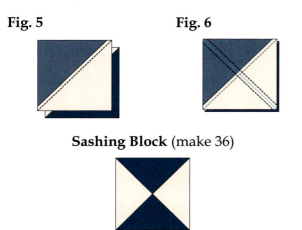

Sashing Block (make 36)

Sew 6 **Blocks** and 5 **sashing strips** together to make **Row**. Make 6 **Rows**.

Row (make 6)

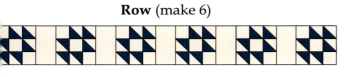

8. Sew 6 **sashing strips** and 5 **Sashing Blocks** together to make **Sashing Row**. Make 7 **Sashing Rows**.

Sashing Row (make 7)

9. Referring to **Quilt Top Diagram**, page 81, sew **Sashing Rows** and **Rows** together to make center section of quilt top.
10. Sew **top**, **bottom**, then **side inner borders** to center section.
11. Place 1 **small square** on 1 **small rectangle** and stitch diagonally (**Fig. 7**). Trim ¼" from stitching (**Fig. 8**) and press open, pressing seam allowance toward darker fabric. Repeat for remaining **small rectangles**.

Fig. 7   **Fig. 8**

12. Place 1 **small square** on opposite end of 1 **small rectangle** and stitch diagonally (**Fig. 9**). Trim ¼" from stitching (**Fig. 10**) and press open, pressing seam allowance toward darker fabric to make **Border Unit**. Repeat to make a total of 116 **Border Units**.

Fig. 9   **Fig. 10**

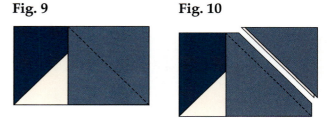

Border Unit (make 116)

13. Sew 28 **Border Units** together to make **Top Pieced Border**. Repeat to make **Bottom Pieced Border**.

Top/Bottom Pieced Border (make 2)

14. Referring to **Fig. 11**, trim off each end of **Top/Bottom Pieced Borders** 1/4" from center of white triangle.

Fig. 11

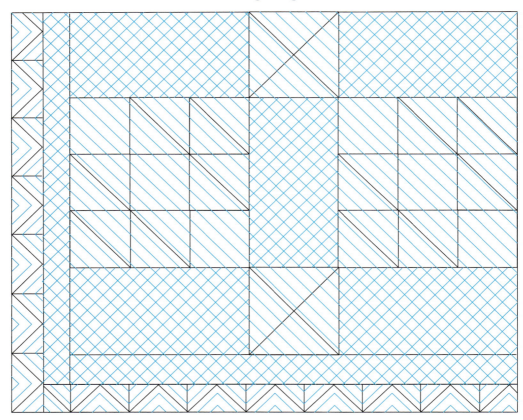

15. Sew 30 **Border Units** together to make **Side Pieced Border**. Make 2 **Side Pieced Borders**.

Side Pieced Border (make 2)

16. Referring to **Quilt Top Diagram**, sew **Top** and **Bottom Pieced Borders**, then **Side Pieced Borders** to center section to complete **Quilt Top**.

COMPLETING THE QUILT

1. Follow **Quilting**, page 151, to mark, layer, and quilt, using **Quilting Diagram** as a suggestion. Our quilt is hand quilted.
2. Cut a 32" square of binding fabric. Follow **Binding**, page 155, to bind quilt using 2 1/2"w bias binding with mitered corners.

Quilting Diagram

Quilt Top Diagram

ALL-AMERICAN COLLECTION

When school's out and summer's in, children and grown-ups alike prepare for a season of breezy, carefree days. And our All-American Collection can help you celebrate those days in red, white, and blue style! Sewn in traditional blue and white, this Ocean Waves quilt is given a patriotic look with bold red blocks. The triangle "tides" are pieced using our simple and accurate grid method, and the open red blocks provide a dramatic background for wave-patterned quilting. You won't want to hide this showpiece away in the guest room — it makes a great picnic spread or tablecloth, too!

To create coordinating accessories for our collection, we echoed the quilt's red, white, and blue color scheme. This picturesque Schoolhouse wall hanging (below) has a quick-to-piece Sawtooth border that's made using the same fast grid technique as the quilt. Each Schoolhouse block is easy to assemble using strip-cut units and pieces cut from basic template shapes. (Opposite) A navy blue border lends a crisp look to the Schoolhouse pillow, and the nautical curtain tiebacks are simply rows of easy-to-piece triangle-squares.

OCEAN WAVES QUILT

SKILL LEVEL: 1 2 3 4 5
BLOCK SIZE: 8" x 8"
QUILT SIZE: 87" x 95"

YARDAGE REQUIREMENTS

Yardage is based on 45"w fabric.

- 6³/₄ yds of navy solid
- 5¹/₄ yds of white solid
- 2¹/₈ yds of red solid
  8 yds for backing
  1 yd for binding
  120" x 120" batting

CUTTING OUT THE PIECES

*All measurements include a ¼" seam allowance. Follow **Rotary Cutting**, page 144, to cut fabric.*

1. **From navy solid:**
    - Cut 8 strips 2⁷/₈"w. From these strips, cut 110 squares 2⁷/₈" x 2⁷/₈". Cut squares once diagonally to make 220 **small triangles**.
    - Cut 2 lengthwise strips 3¹/₂" x 98" for **side borders**.
    - Cut 2 lengthwise strips 3¹/₂" x 84" for **top/bottom borders**.
    - From remaining fabric, cut 14 **rectangles** 19" x 22" for triangle-squares.

2. **From white solid:** ☐
    - Cut 8 strips 2⁷/₈"w. From these strips, cut 110 squares 2⁷/₈" x 2⁷/₈". Cut squares once diagonally to make 220 **small triangles**.
    - Cut 14 **rectangles** 19" x 22" for triangle-squares.

3. **From red solid:** ■
    - Cut 2 strips 9¹/₄"w. From these strips, cut 5 squares 9¹/₄" x 9¹/₄". Cut squares twice diagonally to make 20 **large triangles** (you will need 19 and have 1 left over).
    - Cut 8 strips 6¹/₈"w. From these strips, cut 45 **squares** 6¹/₈" x 6¹/₈".
    - Cut 1 square 4⁷/₈" x 4⁷/₈". Cut square once diagonally to make 2 **corner triangles**.

ASSEMBLING THE QUILT TOP

*Follow **Piecing and Pressing**, page 146, to make quilt top.*

1. To make triangle-squares, place 1 white and 1 navy **rectangle** right sides together. Referring to **Fig. 1**, follow Steps 1 - 3 of **Making Triangle-Squares**, page 147, to draw a grid of 42 squares 2⁷/₈" x 2⁷/₈". Referring to **Fig. 2** for stitching direction, follow Steps 4 - 6 of **Making Triangle-Squares** to make 84 **triangle-squares**. Repeat with remaining rectangles to make a total of 1,176 **triangle-squares** (you will need 1,100 and have 76 left over).

Fig. 1

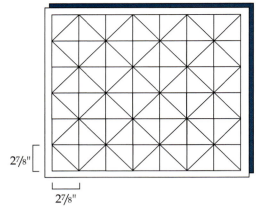

Fig. 2

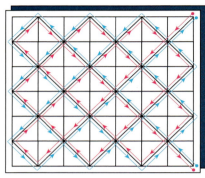

triangle-square (make 1,176)

2. Sew 4 **triangle-squares** together to make **Unit 1**. Make 220 **Unit 1's**.

Unit 1 (make 220)

3. Sew 4 **Unit 1's** together to make **Block A**. Make 20 **Block A's**.

Block A (make 20)

Sew 4 **Unit 1's** together to make **Block B**. Make 25 **Block B's**.

Block B (make 25)

Sew 2 **Unit 1's** together to make **Block C**. Make 14 **Block C's**.

Block C (make 14)

Sew 2 **Unit 1's** together to make **Block D**. Make 5 **Block D's**.

Block D (make 5)

Sew 1 **triangle-square** and 2 **small triangles** together to make **Unit 2**. Make 110 **Unit 2's**.

Unit 2 (make 110)

Sew 1 **triangle-square** and 2 **small triangles** together to make **Unit 3**. Make 110 **Unit 3's**.

Unit 3 (make 110)

9. Sew 2 **Unit 2's**, 2 **Unit 3's**, and 1 **square** together to make **Block E**. Make 45 **Block E's**.

Block E (make 45)

10. Sew 1 **Unit 3**, 1 **large triangle**, and 1 **Unit 2** together to make **Block F**. Make 15 **Block F's**.

Block F (make 15)

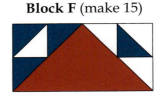

11. Sew 1 **Unit 3**, 1 **large triangle**, and 1 **Unit 2** together to make **Block G**. Make 4 **Block G's**.

Block G (make 4)

12. Sew 1 **corner triangle** and 1 **Unit 2** together to make 1 **Block H**. Sew 1 **corner triangle** and 1 **Unit 3** together to make 1 **Block I**.

Block H (make 1)   **Block I** (make 1)

13. Sew **Block H**, 5 **Block D's**, 4 **Block G's**, and **Block I** together to make 1 **Row A**.

Row A (make 1)

14. Sew 2 **Block C's**, 5 **Block E's**, and 4 **Block A's** together to make **Row B**. Make 5 **Row B's**.

Row B (make 5)

15. Sew 2 **Block F's**, 5 **Block B's**, and 4 **Block E's** together to make **Row C**. Make 5 **Row C's**.

Row C (make 5)

16. Sew 2 **Unit 1's**, 5 **Block F's**, and 4 **Block C's** together to make 1 **Row D**.

Row D (make 1)

17. Referring to **Quilt Top Diagram**, sew **Rows** together to make center section of quilt top.

18. Follow **Adding Squared Borders**, page 150, to sew **top**, **bottom**, then **side borders** to center section to complete **Quilt Top**.

COMPLETING THE QUILT

1. Follow **Quilting**, page 151, to mark, layer, and quilt, using **Quilting Diagram** as a suggestion. Our quilt is hand quilted.

2. Cut a 32" square of binding fabric. Follow **Binding**, page 155, to bind quilt using 2$\frac{1}{2}$"w bias binding with mitered corners.

Quilt Top Diagram

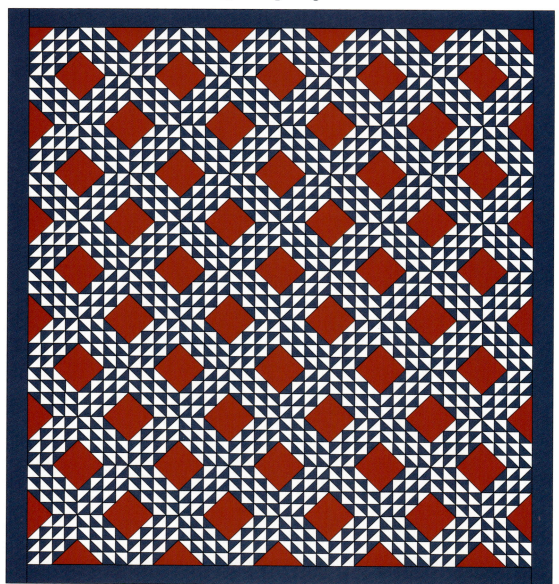

Quilting Diagram

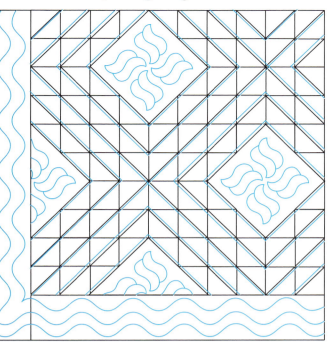

SCHOOLHOUSE WALL HANGING

SKILL LEVEL: 1 2 3 4 5
BLOCK SIZE: 10" x 10"
WALL HANGING SIZE: 44" x 44"

YARDAGE REQUIREMENTS
Yardage is based on 45"w fabric.

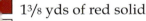 1³/₈ yds of red solid

1³/₈ yds of cream solid
2³/₄ yds for backing and hanging sleeve
³/₄ yd for binding
48" x 48" batting

CUTTING OUT THE PIECES
*All measurements include a ¹/₄" seam allowance. Follow
Rotary Cutting, page 144, to cut fabric unless otherwise
indicated. Label pieces for easy identification.*

- **From red solid:**
  - Cut 2 **side outer borders** 3" x 43".
  - Cut 2 **top/bottom outer borders** 3" x 38".
  - Cut 1 **rectangle** 15" x 22" for triangle-squares.
  - Cut 8 **B's** 1⁵/₈" x 3¹/₈".
  - Cut 4 **C's** 2¹/₂" x 4¹/₈".
  - Cut 4 **D's** 1³/₄" x 4¹/₈".
  - Cut 12 **F's** 1³/₈" x 3¹/₈".
  - Cut 4 **H's** 1¹/₂" x 5⁷/₈".
  - Cut 4 **I's** 1³/₄" x 5⁷/₈".
  - Cut 8 **M's** 1¹/₂" x 1¹/₂".
  - Use patterns, page 93, and follow **Template Cutting**, page 146, to cut 4 **J's** and 4 **L's**.

2. **From cream solid:**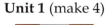
   - Cut 2 **side inner borders** 3" x 38".
   - Cut 2 **top/bottom inner borders** 3" x 33".
   - Cut 3 **long sashing strips** 3" x 28".
   - Cut 6 **short sashing strips** 3" x 10¹/₂".
   - Cut 1 **rectangle** 15" x 22" for triangle-squares.
   - Cut 12 **A's** 1⁷/₈" x 3¹/₈".
   - Cut 4 **E's** 1¹/₂" x 6³/₈".
   - Cut 4 **G's** 1¹/₂" x 5⁷/₈".
   - Cut 4 **N's** 1¹/₂" x 4⁷/₈".
   - Use patterns, page 93, and follow **Template Cutting**, page 146, to cut 8 **O's** (4 in reverse) and 4 **K's**.

ASSEMBLING THE WALL HANGING TOP
*Follow **Piecing and Pressing**, page 146, to assemble wall hanging top.*

1. Sew 2 **B's** and 1 **A** together to make **Unit 1**. Make 4 **Unit 1's**.

Unit 1 (make 4)

2. Sew 1 **Unit 1**, 1 **C**, 1 **D**, and 1 **E** together to make **Unit 2**. Make 4 **Unit 2's**.

Unit 2 (make 4)

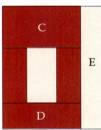

3. Sew 3 **F's** and 2 **A's** together to make **Unit 3**. Make 4 **Unit 3's**.

Unit 3 (make 4)

4. Sew 1 **G**, 1 **H**, 1 **Unit 3**, and 1 **I** together to make **Unit 4**. Make 4 **Unit 4's**.

Unit 4 (make 4)

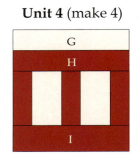

5. Sew 1 **Unit 2** and 1 **Unit 4** together to make **Unit 5**. Make 4 **Unit 5's**.

Unit 5 (make 4)

6. Sew 1 **J**, 1 **K**, and 1 **L** together to make **Unit 6**. Make 4 **Unit 6's**.

Unit 6 (make 4)

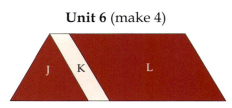

7. Sew 2 **M's** and 1 **N** together to make **Unit 7**. Make 4 **Unit 7's**.

Unit 7 (make 4)

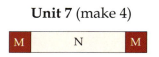

8. Sew 1 **Unit 6** and 1 **Unit 7** together to make **Unit 8**. Make 4 **Unit 8's**.

Unit 8 (make 4)

9. Sew 1 **Unit 8** and 2 **O's** (1 in reverse) together to make **Unit 9**. Make 4 **Unit 9's**.

Unit 9 (make 4)

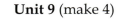

10. Sew 1 **Unit 5** and 1 **Unit 9** together to make **Block**. Make 4 **Blocks**.

Block (make 4)

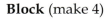

11. Sew 3 **short sashing strips** and 2 **Blocks** together to make **Row**. Make 2 **Rows**.

Row (make 2)

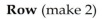

12. Referring to **Wall Hanging Top Diagram**, sew **long sashing strips** and **Rows** together to make center section of wall hanging top.
13. To make triangle-squares, place cream and red **rectangles** right sides together. Referring to **Fig. 1**, follow Steps 1 - 3 of **Making Triangle-Squares**, page 147, to draw a grid of 24 squares $3^3/8$" x $3^3/8$". Referring to **Fig. 2** for stitching direction, follow Steps 4 - 6 of **Making Triangle-Squares** to make a total of 48 **triangle-squares**.

Fig. 1

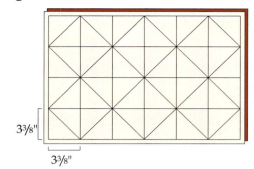

3⅜"

3⅜"

Fig. 2

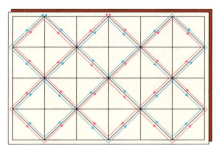

triangle-square (make 48)

Wall Hanging Top Diagram

4. Sew 11 **triangle-squares** together to make each **Top/Bottom Pieced Border**. Sew 13 **triangle-squares** together to make each **Side Pieced Border**.

Top/Bottom Pieced Border (make 2)

Side Pieced Border (make 2)

5. Referring to **Wall Hanging Top Diagram**, sew **Top**, **Bottom**, then **Side Pieced Borders** to center section of wall hanging top.

6. Sew **top**, **bottom**, then **side inner borders** to center section. Repeat with **outer borders** to complete **Wall Hanging Top**.

COMPLETING THE WALL HANGING

- Follow **Quilting**, page 151, to mark, layer, and quilt, using **Quilting Diagram** as a suggestion. Our wall hanging is hand quilted.
- Follow **Making a Hanging Sleeve**, page 157, to attach hanging sleeve.
- Cut a 24" square of binding fabric. Follow **Binding**, page 155, to bind wall hanging using 2½"w bias binding with mitered corners.

Quilting Diagram

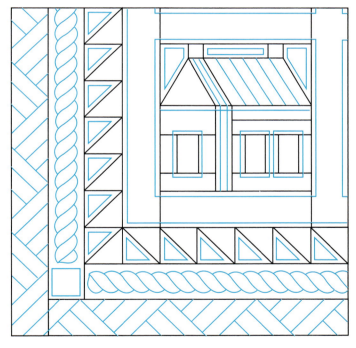

SCHOOLHOUSE PILLOW

PILLOW SIZE: 18" x 18"

YARDAGE REQUIREMENTS

Yardage is based on 45"w fabric.

1/4 yd of red solid
1/4 yd of cream solid
1/8 yd of navy solid
5/8 yd for pillow top backing and pillow back
1/4 yd for binding
22" x 22" batting

You will also need:
polyester fiberfill

CUTTING OUT THE PIECES

*All measurements include a 1/4" seam allowance. Follow **Rotary Cutting**, page 144, to cut fabric unless otherwise indicated.*

1. **From red solid:**
   - Follow Step 1 of **Cutting Out the Pieces** for **Schoolhouse Wall Hanging**, page 89, to cut the following:

2 **B's**	3 **F's**	2 **M's**
1 **C**	1 **H**	1 **J**
1 **D**	1 **I**	1 **L**

2. **From cream solid:**
   - Cut 2 **top/bottom outer borders** 3" x 12 1/2".
   - Cut 2 **side outer borders** 3" x 17 1/2".
   - Follow Step 2 of **Cutting Out the Pieces** for **Schoolhouse Wall Hanging**, page 89, to cut the following:

3 **A's**	1 **G**	2 **O's** (1 in reverse)
1 **E**	1 **N**	1 **K**

3. **From navy solid:**
   - Cut 2 **top/bottom inner borders** 1 1/2" x 10 1/2".
   - Cut 2 **side inner borders** 1 1/2" x 12 1/2".

MAKING THE PILLOW

*Follow **Piecing and Pressing**, page 146, to make pillow.*

1. Follow Steps 1 - 10 of **Assembling the Wall Hanging Top** for **Schoolhouse Wall Hanging**, page 89, to make 1 **Block**.
2. Sew **top**, **bottom**, then **side inner borders** to **Block**. Repeat to add **outer borders**.
3. Follow **Quilting**, page 151, to mark, layer, and quilt, using **Quilting Diagram**, page 91, as a suggestion. Our pillow top is hand quilted.
4. Trim batting and backing even with pillow top edges. Cut pillow back same size as pillow top. Place pillow top and pillow back wrong sides together. Sew pieces together, leaving an opening for stuffing.
5. Stuff pillow with fiberfill and sew opening closed. Follow **Binding**, page 155, to bind pillow edges using 2 1/2"w straight-grain binding with mitered corners.

CURTAIN TIEBACKS

TIEBACK SIZE: 5" x 24"

SUPPLIES

1 fat quarter (18" x 22" piece) **each** of navy solid and cream solid fabric
1/2 yd of 45"w red solid fabric
3/8 yd of 44"w lightweight fleece
4 small cabone (drapery) rings

MAKING THE TIEBACKS

1. To make triangle-squares, place navy and cream fat quarters right sides together. Referring to **Fig.** page 91, follow Steps 1 - 3 of **Making Triangle-Squares**, page 147, to draw a grid of 24 squares 2 7/8" x 2 7/8". Referring to **Fig. 2**, page 91, for stitching direction, follow Steps 4 - 6 of **Making Triangle-Squares** to make 48 triangle-squares.
2. Sew 24 **triangle-squares** together to make each **Tieback Top**.

Tieback Tops

3. Cut 2 strips 6 1/2" x 24 1/2" from red solid for backing. Cut 2 strips 4 1/2" x 24 1/2" from fleece.
4. Place 1 **Tieback Top**, right side up, on 1 fleece strip. Place 1 red backing strip on top of tieback, right sides together. Matching long edges, sew tieback and backing strip together along long edges using a 1/4" seam allowance (backing strip wider than tieback top).
5. Flatten tieback so that tieback top is centered on backing; stitch across 1 end.
6. Turn right side out and press. Turn raw edges of remaining end 1/4" to inside and blindstitch in place.
7. Repeat Steps 4 - 6 for remaining tieback top.
8. Sew 1 ring to backing at each end of tiebacks.

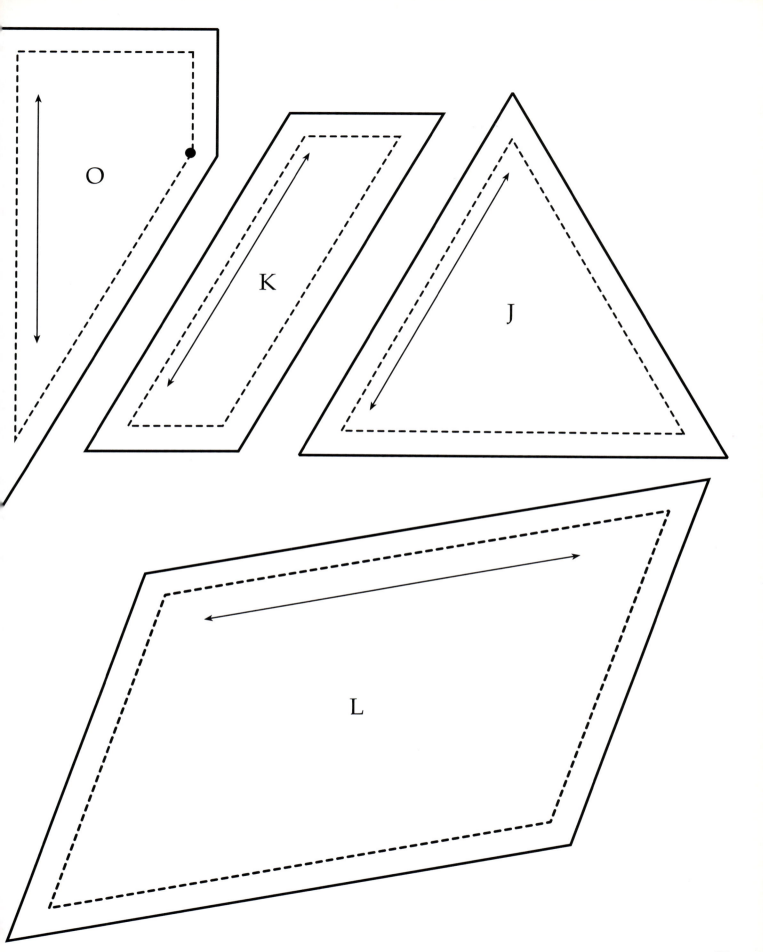

O

K

J

L

SPRINGTIME BABY QUILT

Pieced with love, our Springtime Baby Quilt will welcome a new addition to the family. For quick appliqués, we fused the hearts, flowers, and leaves onto fabric panels and machine stitched the edges of the motifs with clear nylon thread, so there's no need to change thread colors to match all the different fabrics. We used fabric paint to stencil the vines in place! The appliquéd panels are complemented by colorful strip-pieced checkerboard rows. So easy to sew, this project will appeal to novice and experienced quilters.

SPRINGTIME BABY QUILT

SKILL LEVEL: 1 2 3 4 5
QUILT SIZE: 41" x 51"

YARDAGE REQUIREMENTS

Yardage is based on 45"w fabric.

- ☐ 1¾ yds of white print
- ▨ ⅜ yd of yellow check
- ▨ ¼ yd of green stripe
- ◪ ¼ yd **each** of purple check, stripe, and dot
- 2¾ yds for backing
- ¾ yd for binding
- 48" x 60" batting

You will also need:
- paper-backed fusible web
- transparent monofilament thread for appliqué
- plastic template material
- craft knife
- green fabric paint
- stencil brush

CUTTING OUT THE PIECES

All measurements include a ¼" seam allowance. Follow Rotary Cutting, page 144, to cut fabric.

1. **From white print:** ☐
   - Cut 2 **strips** 2½"w.
   - Cut 2 **side outer borders** 6½" x 36½".
   - Cut 2 **top/bottom outer borders** 6½" x 26½".
   - Cut 2 **panels** 9½" x 26½".

2. **From yellow check:** ▨
   - Cut 4 **strips** 2½"w.

3. **From green stripe:** ▨
   - Cut 1 strip 1¼"w. From this strip, cut 4 **border pieces** 1¼" x 6½".
   - Cut 2 **top/bottom inner borders** 1¼" x 40".
   - Cut 2 **side inner borders** 1¼" x 36½".

4. **From purple check, stripe, and dot:** ◪
   - Cut 2 **strips** 2½"w from **each** fabric.

ASSEMBLING THE QUILT TOP

Follow Piecing and Pressing, page 146, to make quilt top.

1. (**Note:** Measurements for stencil placement on **Quilt Top Diagram** do not include seam allowances.) Referring to **Quilt Top Diagram**, use **Stem Stencil** pattern and follow **Stenciling**, page 158, to stencil stems on **outer borders**. Stencil stems on **panels**, using only 2 segments of stem stencil for each design area.

2. Use patterns and follow Steps 1 - 3 of **Invisible Appliqué**, page 148, to cut 10 **Hearts** and 2 **Flower Petals** from purple check, 4 **Flower Petals** from purple stripe, 2 **Flower Petals** from purple dot, 4 **Flower Petals** from yellow check, and 32 **Leaves** and 4 **Flower Bases** from green

stripe. Follow Steps 4 - 14 of **Invisible Appliqué** to stitch appliqués to **panels** and **outer borders**.

3. Sew purple dot and yellow check **strips** together to make **Strip Set A**. Make 2 **Strip Set A's**. Cut across **Strip Set A's** at 2½" intervals to make 29 **Unit 1's**. Repeat with purple check, white print, and purple stripe to make 2 **Strip Set B's** and 22 **Unit 2's**.

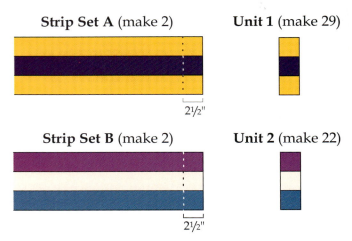

Strip Set A (make 2)   **Unit 1** (make 29)

2½"

Strip Set B (make 2)   **Unit 2** (make 22)

2½"

4. Sew 7 **Unit 1's** and 6 **Unit 2's** together to make **Row**. Make 3 **Rows**.

Row (make 3)

5. Sew 2 **Unit 1's** and 1 **Unit 2** together to make **Border Square**. Make 4 **Border Squares**.

Border Square (make 4)

6. Referring to **Quilt Top Diagram**, sew **Rows** and **panels** together to make center section of quilt top.
7. Sew **side inner borders**, then **side outer borders** to center section.
8. Sew 2 **Border Squares**, 2 **border pieces**, and 1 **top/bottom outer border** together to make **Border Unit**. Make 2 **Border Units**.
9. Sew **top/bottom inner borders**, then **Border Units** to center section to complete **Quilt Top**.

COMPLETING THE QUILT

1. Follow **Quilting**, page 151, to mark, layer, and quilt, using **Quilting Diagram** as a suggestion. Our quilt is hand quilted.

Follow **Binding**, page 155, to bind quilt using 4"w straight-grain binding with overlapped corners.

Quilting Diagram

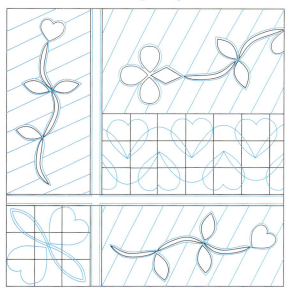

Quilt Top Diagram

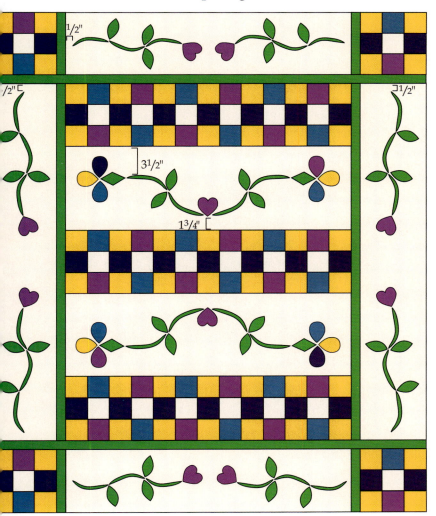

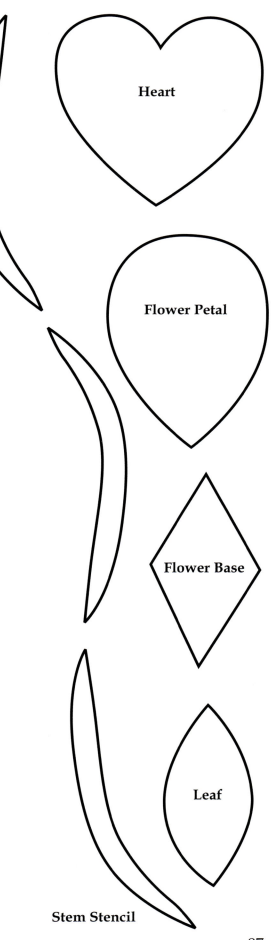

Heart

Flower Petal

Flower Base

Leaf

Stem Stencil

AUTUMN BLOOMS COLLECTION

As lush green summer landscapes change to the fiery hues of fall, we welcome the last vibrant blooms of the year. Clusters of bright gold and deep crimson flowers dot the fields and gardens around our homes. That natural beauty can be enjoyed throughout the year with the richly colored motifs in our Autumn Blooms Collection, which includes a trio of miniature wall decorations and fresh ideas for embellished clothing. The simple appliqué pieces, like those on our flowerpot wall hanging, are fast to assemble using paper-backed fusible web — no stitching is needed! Enhanced with a small amount of simple quilting, this decorative piece couldn't be easier to complete.

A combination of fast appliqué and piecing techniques makes it easy to create our basket medallion wall hanging (right) and sampler-style wall hanging (below). For each of the baskets, we used a simple grid method to sew the triangle-squares. We fused all the appliqué motifs in place.

(Opposite) Choose your favorite floral patterns to easily embellish a knit vest or a crisp cotton shirt. The vest appliqués are quick to fuse in place, and the mock patch pockets are sewn on with embroidery floss. A gardener's delight, the shirt blooms with fused-on fabric flowers and sewn-on trim.

BASKET WALL HANGING

SKILL LEVEL: 1 2 3 4 5
BLOCK SIZE: 4 1/2" x 4 1/2"
WALL HANGING SIZE: 14" x 14"

YARDAGE REQUIREMENTS

Yardage is based on 45"w fabric.

1/4 yd of brown plaid
1/4 yd of dark brown print
1/4 yd of tan print
1/4 yd of tan check
scrap of rust print for basket handles
scraps of floral prints for flowers in baskets
1/2 yd for backing and hanging sleeve
1/4 yd for binding
16" x 16" batting

You will also need:
heavy-duty paper-backed fusible web

CUTTING OUT THE PIECES

*All measurements include a 1/4" seam allowance. Follow **Rotary Cutting**, page 144, to cut fabric unless otherwise indicated.*

1. **From brown plaid:**
   - Cut 2 squares 7 1/4" x 7 1/4". Cut squares once diagonally to make 4 **setting triangles**.
2. **From dark brown print:**
   - Cut 1 strip 1 5/8"w. From this strip, cut 14 squares 1 5/8" x 1 5/8". Cut squares once diagonally to make 28 **triangles**.
   - Cut 1 **rectangle** 6" x 11" for triangle-squares.
3. **From tan print:**
   - Cut 1 **rectangle** 6" x 11" for triangle-squares.
   - Cut 4 **squares** 1 1/4" x 1 1/4".
4. **From tan check:**
   - Cut 1 strip 1 1/4"w. From this strip, cut 8 **rectangles** 1 1/4" x 3 1/2".
   - Cut 2 squares 4 5/8" x 4 5/8". Cut squares once diagonally to make 4 **large triangles**.
   - Cut 2 squares 2 3/8" x 2 3/8". Cut squares once diagonally to make 4 **medium triangles**.
5. **From scrap of rust print:**
   - Use pattern **A**, page 107, and follow Steps 1 - 3 of **Invisible Appliqué**, page 148, to cut out 4 **basket handles**.
6. **From scraps of floral prints:**
   - Fuse web to wrong side of fabric scraps. Cut out desired **flowers**, taking advantage of fabric design. Remove paper backing.

ASSEMBLING THE WALL HANGING TOP

*Follow **Piecing and Pressing**, page 146, to make wall hanging top.*

1. To make triangle-squares, place dark brown and tan print **rectangles** right sides together. Referring to **Fig. 1**, follow **Making Triangle-Squares**, page 147, to complete 36 **triangle-squares**.

Fig. 1

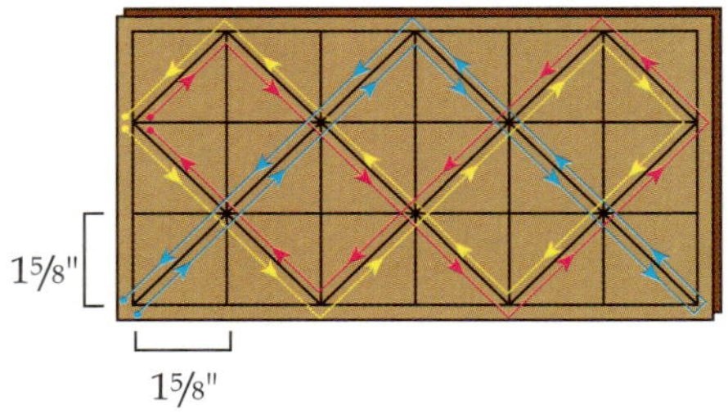
1 5/8"
1 5/8"

triangle-square (make 36)

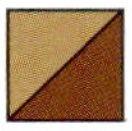

2. Sew 9 **triangle-squares**, 5 **triangles**, and 1 **square** together to make **Rows A**, **B**, **C**, **D**, and **E**. Sew **Rows** together to make **Unit 1**. Make 4 **Unit 1's**.

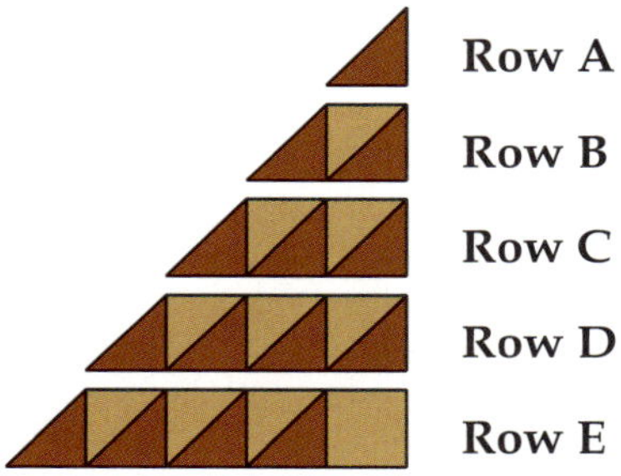
Row A
Row B
Row C
Row D
Row E

Unit 1 (make 4)

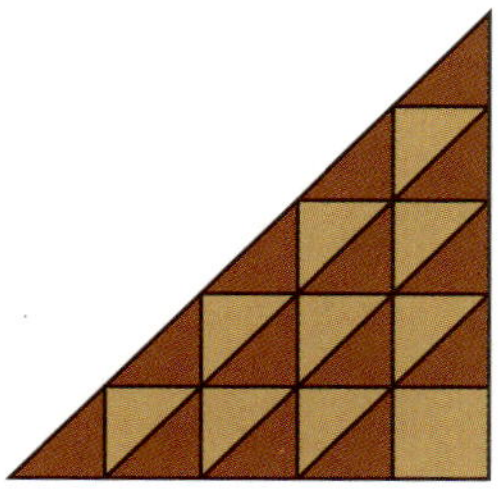

3. Referring to **Wall Hanging Top Diagram**, fuse **basket handles** to **large triangles**, making sure ends of handles extend into seam allowance.
4. Sew 1 **Unit 1** and 1 **large triangle** together to make **Unit 2**. Make 4 **Unit 2's**.

Unit 2 (make 4)

Sew 1 **rectangle** and 1 **triangle** together to make **Unit 3**. Make 4 **Unit 3's**. Sew 1 **triangle** and 1 **rectangle** together to make **Unit 4**. Make 4 **Unit 4's**.

Unit 3 (make 4)   **Unit 4** (make 4)

   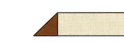

Sew 1 **Unit 2**, 1 **Unit 3**, 1 **Unit 4**, and 1 **medium triangle** together to make **Basket Block**. Make 4 **Basket Blocks**.

Basket Block (make 4)

- Referring to photo, fuse **flowers** to **Basket Blocks**.
- Referring to **Wall Hanging Top Diagram**, sew **Basket Blocks** together to make center section of wall hanging top.
- Sew **setting triangles** to center section to complete **Wall Hanging Top**.

COMPLETING THE WALL HANGING
- Follow **Quilting**, page 151, to mark, layer, and quilt, using **Quilting Diagram** as a suggestion. Our wall hanging is hand quilted.
- Follow **Making a Hanging Sleeve**, page 157, to attach hanging sleeve to wall hanging.
- Follow **Binding**, page 155, to bind wall hanging using 2"w straight-grain binding with mitered corners.

Wall Hanging Top Diagram

Quilting Diagram

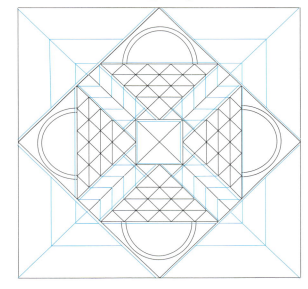

FLOWERPOT WALL HANGING

SKILL LEVEL: 1 2 3 4 5
WALL HANGING SIZE: 10" x 15"

YARDAGE REQUIREMENTS
Yardage is based on 45"w fabric.

   ¼ yd of tan check
   ¼ yd of gold print
   ⅛ yd of brown plaid
   scraps of assorted prints for appliqués

1/4 yd for binding
3/8 yd for backing and hanging sleeve
13" x 19" batting

You will also need:
heavy-duty paper-backed fusible web

CUTTING OUT THE PIECES

All measurements include a 1/4" seam allowance. Follow Rotary Cutting, page 144, to cut fabric unless otherwise indicated.

1. **From tan check:**
    - Cut 1 **background** 6½" x 13¼".

2. **From gold print:**
    - Cut 2 strips 1½"w. From these strips, cut 2 **top/bottom borders** 1½" x 13¼" and 2 **side borders** 1½" x 9½".

3. **From brown plaid:**
    - Cut 1 **strip** 1½" x 13¼".

4. **From scraps of assorted prints:**
    - Referring to photo, use patterns, page 107, and follow Steps 1 - 3 of **Invisible Appliqué**, page 148, to cut out desired **appliqués**. (We used patterns **B - Y** for our wall hanging.)

ASSEMBLING THE WALL HANGING TOP

Follow Piecing and Pressing, page 146, and refer to photo to make wall hanging top.

1. Sew **strip** to **background** to make center section of wall hanging top.
2. Sew **top**, **bottom**, then **side borders** to center section.
3. Follow manufacturer's instructions to fuse **appliqués** to center section to complete **Wall Hanging Top**.

COMPLETING THE WALL HANGING

1. Follow **Quilting**, page 151, to mark, layer, and quilt. Our wall hanging is hand quilted in the ditch along inner edge of border.
2. Follow **Making a Hanging Sleeve**, page 157, to attach hanging sleeve to wall hanging.
3. Follow **Binding**, page 155, to bind wall hanging using 2"w straight-grain binding with mitered corners.

SAMPLER WALL HANGING

SKILL LEVEL: 1 2 3 4 5
WALL HANGING SIZE: 15" x 15"

YARDAGE REQUIREMENTS

Yardage is based on 45"w fabric.

- 1/4 yd of light tan print for background
- 1/4 yd of rust print
- 1/4 yd of dark rust print
- 1/4 yd of dark gold plaid
- 1/4 yd of tan print

  scraps of assorted prints for flower and flowerpot appliqués
  5/8 yd for backing and hanging sleeve
  1/4 yd for binding
  18" x 18" batting

You will also need:
heavy-duty paper-backed fusible web

CUTTING OUT THE PIECES

All measurements include a 1/4" seam allowance. Follow Rotary Cutting, page 144, to cut fabric unless otherwise indicated.

1. **From light tan print:**
    - Cut 1 **A** 3¾" x 4½".
    - Cut 1 **C** 3¾" x 3¾".
    - Cut 1 **G** 3¾" x 4¼".
    - Cut 1 square 4⅝" x 4⅝". Cut square once diagonally to make 2 **large triangles** (you will need 1 and have 1 left over).
    - Cut 1 square 2⅜" x 2⅜". Cut square once diagonally to make 2 **small triangles** (you will need 1 and have 1 left over).
    - Cut 2 **rectangles** 1¼" x 3½".

2. **From rust print:**
    - Cut 1 strip 1½"w. From this strip, cut 2 **top/bottom inner borders** 1½" x 9" and 2 **side inner borders** 1½" x 11".
    - Cut 1 **B** 1¼" x 4½".
    - Cut 1 **E** 1¾" x 4½".
    - Cut 1 **F** 1¼" x 3¾".
    - Cut 1 **H** 1¼" x 5".

3. **From dark rust print:**
    - Cut 2 strips 2½"w. From these strips, cut 2 **side outer borders** 2½" x 15" and 2 **top/bottom outer borders** 2½" x 11".

From dark gold plaid:
- Cut 1 **rectangle** 5" x 6" for triangle-squares.
- Cut 4 squares 1⁵/₈" x 1⁵/₈". Cut squares once diagonally to make 8 **triangles** (you will need 7 and have 1 left over).

From tan print:
- Cut 1 **rectangle** 5" x 6" for triangle-squares.
- Cut 1 **square** 1¹/₄" x 1¹/₄".

From scraps of assorted prints:
- Cut 1 **D** 1¹/₄" x 3³/₄".
- Use patterns, page 107, and follow Steps 1 - 3 of **Invisible Appliqué**, page 148, to cut 1 **A** for basket handle and desired **appliqués**. (We used patterns **B** - **Y** for our wall hanging.)

ASSEMBLING THE WALL HANGING TOP

Follow Piecing and Pressing, page 146, to make wall hanging top.

To make triangle-squares, place dark gold and tan print **rectangles** right sides together. Referring to **Fig. 1**, follow **Making Triangle-Squares**, page 147, to make 12 **triangle-squares** (you will need 9 and have 3 left over).

Fig. 1

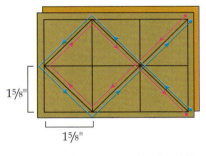

1⁵/₈"

1⁵/₈"

triangle-square (make 12)

- Follow Steps 1 - 6 of **Assembling the Wall Hanging Top** for **Basket Wall Hanging**, page 102, to make 1 **Basket Block**.
- Referring to **Assembly Diagram**, sew **A** and **B** together to make **Unit 1**. Sew **C**, **D**, and **E** together to make **Unit 2**. Sew **F**, **G**, and **H** together to make **Unit 3**.
- Sew **Unit 1**, **Unit 2**, **Unit 3**, and **Basket Block** together to make center section of wall hanging top.
- Referring to photo, follow manufacturer's instructions to fuse **appliqués** to center section.

6. Sew **top**, **bottom**, then **side inner borders** to center section. Repeat with **outer borders** to complete **Wall Hanging Top**.

COMPLETING THE WALL HANGING

1. Follow **Quilting**, page 151, to mark, layer, and quilt, using **Quilting Diagram** as a suggestion. Our quilt is hand quilted.
2. Follow **Making a Hanging Sleeve**, page 157, to attach hanging sleeve to wall hanging.
3. Follow **Binding**, page 155, to bind wall hanging using 2"w straight-grain binding with mitered corners.

Assembly Diagram

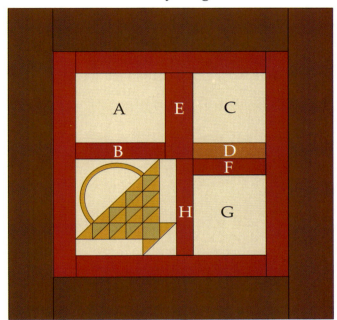

Quilting Diagram

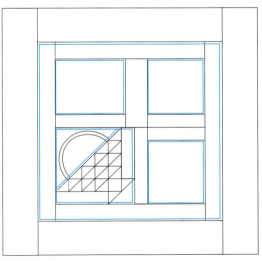

GARDENER'S SHIRT

SUPPLIES
1 shirt
desired fabric for shirt trim
scraps of assorted print fabrics for appliqués
heavy-duty paper-backed fusible web

TRIMMING THE SHIRT
1. Use patterns and follow Steps 1 - 3 of **Invisible Appliqué**, page 148, to cut desired **appliqués** from assorted scraps. (We used patterns **H - M** for our shirt.)
2. Follow manufacturer's instructions to fuse **appliqués** to shirt.
3. To make shirt trim, measure along 1 edge of shirt to be trimmed; add 1". Cut strip of fabric (pieced as necessary) $7/8$"w by the determined measurement. Press ends of strip $1/2$" to wrong side. Press long edges of strip $1/4$" to wrong side. Repeat for remaining edges to be trimmed.
4. Topstitch trim pieces to shirt.

FLOWERPOT VEST

SUPPLIES
1 knit vest
$1/4$ yd of 45"w red check fabric
5" x 12" piece of tan print fabric
scraps of assorted print fabrics for appliqués
embroidery floss
heavy-duty paper-backed fusible web

CUTTING OUT THE PIECES
All measurements include a $1/4$" seam allowance. Follow **Rotary Cutting**, *page 144, to cut fabric unless otherwise indicated.*

1. **From red check fabric:**
   - Cut 2 **patch backing pieces** $5^{1}/4$" x $6^{3}/4$".
   - Cut 4 **top/bottom borders** 1" x $5^{1}/4$".
   - Cut 4 **side borders** 1" x $5^{3}/4$".
2. **From tan print fabric:**
   - Cut 2 **patch backgrounds** $4^{1}/4$" x $5^{3}/4$".
3. **From scraps of assorted print fabrics:**
   - Use patterns and follow Steps 1 - 3 of **Invisible Appliqué**, page 148, to cut out desired **appliqués**. (We used patterns **B - G** and **N - DD** for our vest.)

TRIMMING THE VEST
Follow **Piecing and Pressing**, *page 146, to make patches.*
1. Referring to photo, follow manufacturer's instructions to fuse **appliqués** to **patch backgrounds** and to vest.
2. Sew **side**, then **top** and **bottom borders** to **patch backgrounds** to make patch fronts.
3. Place each patch front and **backing piece** right sides together. Stitch along all edges. To complete patches, cut a slit in center of backing pieces only; turn right side out and press.
4. Stitch patches to vest using 6 strands of floss and a long running stitch. Stitch around armholes and neck edges using floss and a long running stitch.

QUICK TIP

USING FUSIBLE WEB

*Many of us don't have as much time as we'd like to create decorative accents, clothing, and gift projects. As a time-saving idea, some of the projects in our book use fusible web as a substitute for slower handwork. (**Note:** We used Pellon® Wonder-Under™ to secure appliqués that were stitched in place and Heavy-Duty Wonder-Under™ when no stitching was done.) The following tips will help you achieve consistent results when using fusible products.*

- *We recommend using a piece of muslin or scrap cotton fabric to protect your ironing board from excess fusible adhesives. You may wish to use a pressing cloth to protect your iron even if the fusible products you use do not recommend it. It may also be helpful to keep iron cleaner handy for occasional accidents.*

- *Instructions for fusing and recommendations for laundering vary widely among fusible products. We recommend that for each project you use only products with similar fusing and laundering instructions.*

- *When using a fusible product, follow the manufacturer's instructions carefully to ensure a sufficient bond. **Always** test the fusible product you are using on a piece of scrap fabric before making the project, testing the bond and adjusting conditions as recommended by the manufacturer.*

- *If the fusible product you are using does not give satisfactory results, try a different fusible product.*

- *Some fabrics shrink when pressed at high temperatures — especially when using steam. If this occurs when testing your fabric sample and a lower temperature is not sufficient to properly melt the fusible web, choose a different fabric.*

NORTHERN LIGHTS

A romantic picnic lunch is the perfect way to spend a leisurely summer day. And what could complete the comfy setting better than our Northern Lights quilt! Gentle lavender and soft yellow fabrics create a splendid color contrast. If you look closely at the unique design, you'll see that it's created with two basic units — the four-patch block, made from strip sets, and an easy triangle-square, created with a fast grid method. Using a compass or round object, you can create perfectly matched scallops for a fanciful finish.

NORTHERN LIGHTS QUILT

SKILL LEVEL: 1 2 3 4 5
BLOCK SIZE: 7" x 7"
QUILT SIZE: 78" x 92"

YARDAGE REQUIREMENTS
Yardage is based on 45"w fabric.

- 4¹/₈ yds of lavender solid
- 5¹/₄ yds of yellow solid
  7¹/₄ yds for backing
  ⁷/₈ yd for binding
  90" x 108" batting

CUTTING OUT THE PIECES
All measurements include a ¼" seam allowance. Follow Rotary Cutting, page 144, to cut fabric.

1. **From lavender solid:**
    - Cut 28 **strips** 2¹/₄"w.
    - Cut 6 **rectangles** 19" x 23" for triangle-squares.

2. **From yellow solid:**
    - Cut 28 **strips** 2¹/₄"w.
    - Cut 2 lengthwise strips 4" x 84¹/₂" for **side borders**.
    - Cut 2 lengthwise strips 4" x 70¹/₂" for **top/bottom borders**.
    - From remaining fabric, cut 6 **rectangles** 19" x 23" for triangle-squares.

ASSEMBLING THE QUILT TOP
Follow Piecing and Pressing, page 146, to make quilt top.

1. Sew **strips** together to make **Strip Set**. Make 28 **Strip Sets**. Cut across **Strip Sets** at 2¹/₄" intervals to make 488 **Unit 1's**.

Strip Set (make 28)   **Unit 1** (make 488)

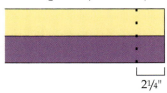

2¹/₄"

2. Sew 2 **Unit 1's** together to make **Unit 2**. Make 244 **Unit 2's**.

Unit 2 (make 244)

3. To make triangle-squares, place 1 lavender and yellow **rectangle** right sides together. Referring to **Fig. 1**, follow Steps 1 - 3 of **Making Triangle-Squares**, page 147, to draw a grid of 20 squares 4³/₈" x 4³/₈". Referring to **Fig. 2** for stitching direction, follow Steps 4 - 6 of **Making Triangle Squares** to complete 40 triangle-squares. Repeat with remaining **rectangles** to make a total of 240 **triangle-squares**.

Fig. 1

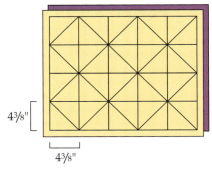

4³/₈"

4³/₈"

Fig. 2

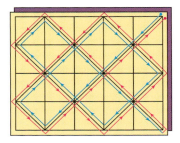

triangle-square (make 240)

4. Sew 2 **Unit 2's** and 2 **triangle-squares** together to make **Block**. Make 120 **Blocks**.

Block (make 120)

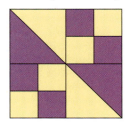

5. Sew 10 **Blocks** together to make **Row**. Make 12 **Rows**.

Row (make 12)

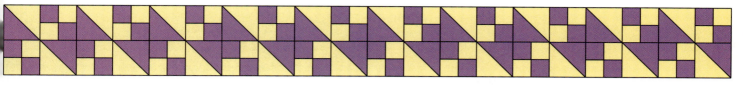

Referring to **Quilt Top Diagram**, page 112, sew **Rows** together to make center section of quilt top.

Sew 1 **Unit 2** to each end of **top** and **bottom borders**. Sew **side**, then **top** and **bottom borders** to center section to complete **Quilt Top**.

COMPLETING THE QUILT

To mark scallops on borders, refer to **Fig. 3** and mark dots 1" from edge of each border at 3½" intervals, using seamlines in **Blocks** as guides. Use a compass or round object to draw scalloped lines connecting dots. Do not trim.

Fig. 3

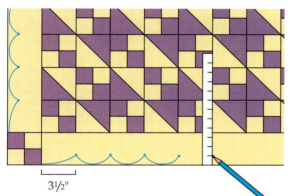

3½"

Follow **Quilting**, page 151, to mark, layer, and quilt, using **Quilting Diagram** as a suggestion. Our quilt is hand quilted using **Quilting Pattern**, page 113.

Cut a 27" square of binding fabric. Follow **Making Continuous Bias Strip Binding**, page 155, to make approximately 14 yds of 1½"w bias binding.

4. Follow Steps 1 and 2 of **Attaching Binding with Mitered Corners**, page 156, and pin binding to front of quilt, matching raw edges of binding to scalloped line. Using a ¼" seam allowance and easing around curves, sew binding to quilt until binding overlaps beginning end by 2"; trim excess binding. Trim quilt top, batting, and backing even with raw edges of binding. Fold binding over to quilt backing and pin in place, covering stitching line. Blindstitch binding to backing.

Quilting Diagram

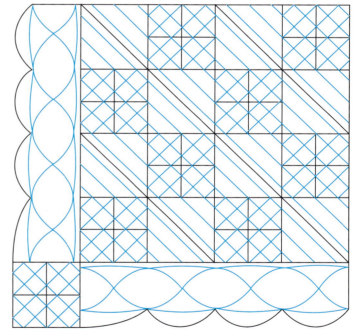

Quilt Top Diagram

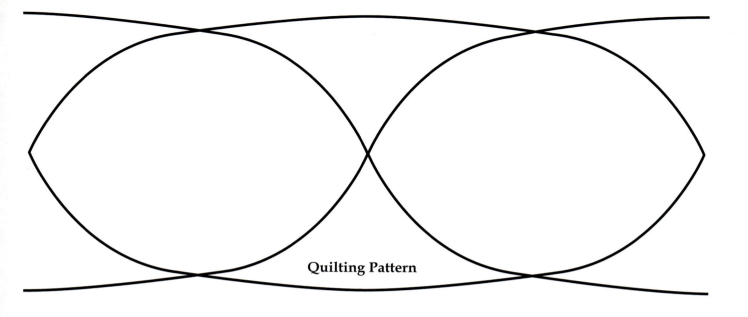

Quilting Pattern

QUICK TIP

USING SINGLE-FOLD BIAS BINDING FOR SCALLOPED EDGES

Our instructions usually recommend French or double-fold bias binding because of its durability. However, for quilts with scalloped edges like our Northern Lights Quilt, page 110, you may find it easier to apply single-fold bias binding, since it is less bulky and may be eased around curves more smoothly.

1. *Single-fold bias binding should be cut approximately twice the width of the desired finished binding plus ½" for seam allowances. You may wish to test the finished width of your binding strips on layered scraps of fabric and batting, since the thickness of your layered quilt will affect the finished width of your binding. A narrower binding will be easier to ease around curves and to apply to the inside points between the scallops than a wider one.*

2. *Press 1 long edge of binding strip ¼" to the wrong side and press 1 end diagonally (see **Fig. 1**) before applying binding to quilt. The long pressed edge will be folded over to the back of the quilt and blindstitched.*

3. *Begin applying binding on as straight an edge as possible, usually near 1 end of a scallop. Do not begin at a corner or inside point. With right sides together, align long raw edge of binding with scalloped line that has been marked on quilt top. Using a scant ¼" seam allowance, stitch binding*

*to quilt, carefully aligning edge of binding with marked line and easing slightly around the outside curves. At inside points between scallops, raise presser foot and pivot quilt; lower presser foot and take 1 stitch straight across the point. Pivot quilt again and continue stitching (**Fig. 1**). Be careful not to allow a pleat or pucker to form at inside point.*

Fig. 1

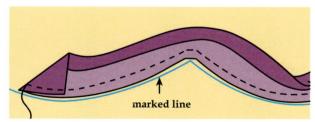

marked line

4. *Continue stitching binding to quilt until binding overlaps beginning end by 1"; trim excess binding. Trim quilt top, batting, and backing even with edge of binding. Clip seam allowance into each point between scallops, taking care not to cut stitching. Fold binding over to quilt backing and blindstitch in place, covering stitching line.*

COUNTRY
CHICKENS
COLLECTION

Quilters have always been inspired by images from their everyday lives. So it's only natural that country stitchers would have incorporated their feathered friends into patchwork patterns. In that tradition, we've assembled our Country Chickens Collection, which features a generous lap quilt and kitchen accessories made using a quaint assortment of homespun plaids and barnyard motifs. The lap quilt, which can also be used as a wall hanging, is easy to make using our simple grid method to create the colorful triangle-squares. For our machine appliqués, we used clear nylon thread to produce a clean edge. And the small size of this quilt means you'll see results as quick as a hen's peck!

ur henhouse-inspired accessories will add a bit of country charm to your kitchen. Featuring a flock of our feathered friends, the table mat (opposite) is bordered with a simple strip-pieced checkerboard. The coordinating chair covers are a fast way to dress up ladder-back chairs. Completing the collection, our home-style pot holders (below) are quick to create — and handy, too! The simple motifs are machine appliquéd and finished with basic in-the-ditch and grid quilting.

ROOSTERS IN A ROW LAP QUILT

SKILL LEVEL: 1 2 3 4 5
BLOCK SIZE: 8" x 8"
QUILT SIZE: 59" x 75"

YARDAGE REQUIREMENTS
Yardage is based on 45"w fabric.

- 2³/₈ yds of green plaid
- 2¹/₄ yds of black solid
- 1¹/₈ yds of light green plaid
- ³/₄ yd of dark green plaid
- ³/₄ yd of tan plaid
- ³/₄ yd of red print
- ³/₄ yd of red stripe
- assorted scraps for appliqués
  3³/₄ yds for backing
  ⁷/₈ yd for binding
  72" x 90" batting

You will also need:
  transparent monofilament thread for appliqué
  paper-backed fusible web

CUTTING OUT THE PIECES
All measurements include a ¼" seam allowance. Follow Rotary Cutting, page 144, to cut fabric unless otherwise indicated.

1. **From green plaid:**
   - Cut 2 lengthwise strips 4¹/₂" x 78" for **side outer borders**.
   - Cut 2 lengthwise strips 4¹/₂" x 54" for **top/bottom outer borders**.

2. **From black solid:**
   - Cut 2 lengthwise strips 1¹/₂" x 70" for **side inner borders**.
   - Cut 2 lengthwise strips 1¹/₂" x 52" for **top/bottom inner borders**.

3. **From light green plaid:**
   - Cut 4 strips 8¹/₂"w. From these strips, cut 16 **squares** 8¹/₂" x 8¹/₂".

4. **From dark green plaid:**
   - Cut 2 **squares** 21" x 21" for triangle-squares.

5. **From tan plaid:**
   - Cut 2 **squares** 21" x 21" for triangle-squares.

6. **From red print:**
   - Cut 2 **squares** 21" x 21" for triangle-squares.

7. **From red stripe:**
   - Cut 2 **squares** 21" x 21" for triangle-squares.

8. **From assorted scraps:**
   - Referring to photo, use patterns, pages 122 - 12[?] and follow Steps 1 - 3 of **Invisible Appliqué**, page 148, to cut out the following **appliqués**[?]
     5 **Bodies**
     5 **Wings**
     5 **Beaks**
     5 **Combs**
     1 **Star**

ASSEMBLING THE QUILT TOP
Follow Piecing and Pressing, page 146, to make quilt to[?]

1. To make green triangle-squares, place 1 dark green plaid and 1 tan plaid **square** right sides together. Referring to **Fig. 1**, follow **Making Triangle-Squares**, page 147, to make 32 **green triangle-squares**. Repeat with remaining dark green and tan plaid **squares** to make a total of 64 **green triangle-squares**. Use red print and re[?] stripe **squares** and repeat to make a total of 64 **red triangle-squares**.

Fig. 1

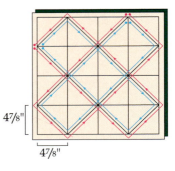

4⁷/₈"
4⁷/₈"

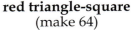

green triangle-square (make 64)   **red triangle-square** (make 64)

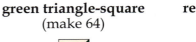

2. Sew 4 **green triangle-squares** together to make[?] **Unit 1**. Make 16 **Unit 1's**. Sew 4 **red triangle-squares** together to make **Unit 2**. Make 16 **Unit 2**[?]

Unit 1 (make 16)   **Unit 2** (make 16)

3. Referring to **Quilt Top Diagram**, follow Steps 4 - 14 of **Invisible Appliqué**, page 149, to stitch **appliqués** to 6 light green plaid **squares** to make 6 **Appliquéd Blocks**.

- Referring to **Quilt Top Diagram**, sew **Unit 1's**, **Unit 2's**, **Appliquéd Blocks**, and remaining **squares** together into rows. Sew rows together to make center section of quilt top.
- Follow **Adding Squared Borders**, page 150, to sew **top**, **bottom**, then **side inner borders** to center section. Repeat with **outer borders** to complete **Quilt Top**.

COMPLETING THE QUILT

- Follow **Quilting**, page 151, to mark, layer, and quilt, using **Quilting Diagram** as a suggestion. Our quilt is hand quilted.
- Cut a 28" square of binding fabric. Follow **Binding**, page 155, to bind quilt using 2^1/$_2$"w bias binding with mitered corners.

Quilting Diagram

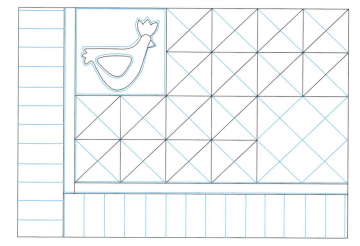

Quilt Top Diagram

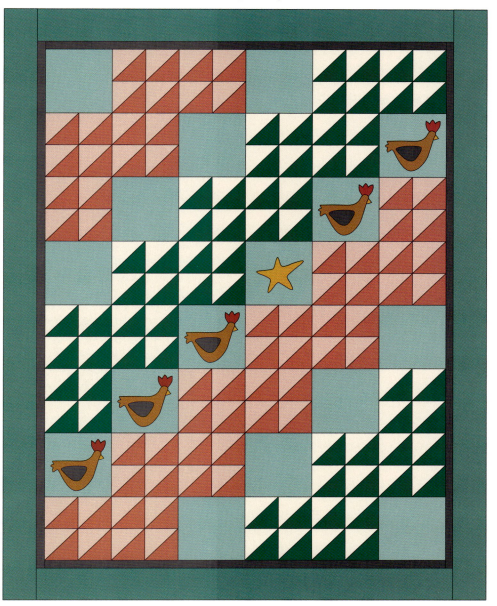

HEN PARTY TABLE MAT

BLOCK SIZE: 9" x 9"
TABLE MAT SIZE: 37" x 37"

YARDAGE REQUIREMENTS

Yardage is based on 45"w fabric.

- ³/₈ yd of red print
- ³/₈ yd of red stripe
- ³/₈ yd of dark red print
- ³/₈ yd of green plaid
- ³/₈ yd of tan plaid
- ¼ yd of black solid
- assorted scraps for appliqués
  1¼ yds for backing
  ³/₈ yd for binding
  45" x 60" batting

You will also need:
   transparent monofilament thread for appliqué
   paper-backed fusible web

CUTTING OUT THE PIECES

All measurements include a ¼" seam allowance. Follow
Rotary Cutting, page 144, to cut fabric unless otherwise
indicated.

1. **From red print:**
   - Cut 4 **strips** 2½"w.
2. **From red stripe:**
   - Cut 4 **strips** 2½"w.
3. **From dark red print:**
   - Cut 4 **large squares** 9½" x 9½".
4. **From green plaid:**
   - Cut 1 **large square** 9½" x 9½".
   - Cut 4 **small squares** 4½" x 4½".
5. **From tan plaid:**
   - Cut 4 **large squares** 9½" x 9½".
6. **From black solid:**
   - Cut 2 **top/bottom borders** 1" x 27½".
   - Cut 2 **side borders** 1" x 28½".
7. **From assorted scraps:**
   - Referring to photo, use patterns, pages 122 - 123, and follow Steps 1 - 3 of **Invisible Appliqué**, page 148, to cut out the following **appliqués:**
     - 4 **Bodies**
     - 4 **Wings**
     - 4 **Beaks**
     - 4 **Combs**
     - 1 **Star**

ASSEMBLING THE TABLE MAT TOP

Follow Piecing and Pressing, page 146, to make table
mat top.

1. Referring to **Table Mat Top Diagram**, follow Steps 4 - 14 of **Invisible Appliqué**, page 149, to stitch **appliqués** to green plaid and tan plaid **large squares** to complete **Appliquéd Blocks**.
2. Sew **Appliquéd Blocks** and remaining **large squares** together into rows. Sew rows together to make center section of table mat top.
3. Sew **top**, **bottom**, then **side borders** to center section.
4. Sew **strips** together to make **Strip Set**. Make 4 **Strip Sets**. Cut across **Strip Sets** at 2½" intervals to make 56 **Unit 1's**.

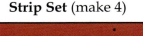
Strip Set (make 4)   **Unit 1** (make 56)

2½"

5. Sew 14 **Unit 1's** together to make **Pieced Border**. Make 4 **Pieced Borders**.

Pieced Border (make 4)

6. Sew **Pieced Borders** to top and bottom of center section. Sew 1 **small square** to each end of remaining **Pieced Borders**. Sew borders to sides of center section to complete **Table Mat Top**.

COMPLETING THE TABLE MAT

1. Follow **Quilting**, page 151, to mark, layer, and quilt, using **Quilting Diagram** as a suggestion. Our table mat is hand quilted.
2. Follow **Binding**, page 155, to bind table mat using 2½"w straight-grain binding with overlapped corners.

Table Mat Top Diagram

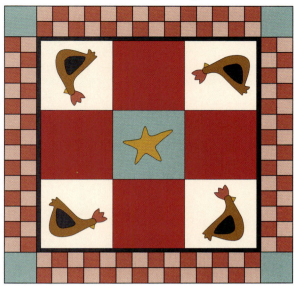

Quilting Diagram

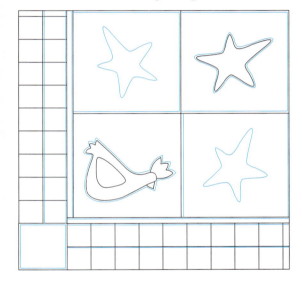

HOME-STYLE POT HOLDERS

POT HOLDER SIZE: 10" x 10"

Instructions are for making 1 pot holder.

YARDAGE REQUIREMENTS
Yardage is based on 45"w fabric.

 1 fat quarter (18" x 22" piece) each of red print and green plaid

⬛ 1/8 yd of black solid

◤ scrap(s) for desired appliqué(s)
12" x 12" square for backing
12" x 12" batting

You will also need:
transparent monofilament thread for appliqué
paper-backed fusible web

CUTTING OUT THE PIECES
*All measurements include a 1/4" seam allowance. Follow **Rotary Cutting**, page 144, to cut fabric unless otherwise indicated.*

1. **From red print and green plaid:** ◤
   - Cut 1 **background square** 8 1/2" x 8 1/2" from 1 fabric.
   - Cut 2 **short borders** 1 1/4" x 8 1/2" and 2 **long borders** 1 1/4" x 10" from remaining fabric.

2. **From black solid:** ⬛
   - Cut 1 **strip** 2 1/4" x 46" for binding, pieced as necessary.

3. **From scrap(s) for desired appliqué(s):** ◤
   - Use patterns, pages 122 - 123, and follow Steps 1 - 3 of **Invisible Appliqué**, page 148, to cut out desired **appliqué(s)**.

MAKING THE POT HOLDER
1. Referring to photo, follow Steps 4 - 14 of **Invisible Appliqué**, page 149, to stitch **appliqué(s)** to **background square**.
2. Sew **short**, then **long borders** to **background square**.
3. Follow **Quilting**, page 151, to mark, layer, and quilt. Our pot holder is hand quilted in the ditch around inside of border and in a diagonal grid (see photo).
4. Trim batting and backing even with edges of pot holder top.
5. For binding, press **strip** in half lengthwise with wrong sides together. Beginning at top corner, follow Steps 2 - 7 of **Attaching Binding with Mitered Corners**, page 156, to attach binding to front of pot holder, leaving excess binding attached for hanging loop. Fold binding over to backing, finger pressing hanging loop so that raw edges are enclosed in binding; pin in place. Blindstitch binding in place. Press end of hanging loop 1/2" to wrong side; fold to back of pot holder and stitch in place.

COCK-A-DOODLE CHAIR COVERS

SIZE: 12" x 31"

Instructions are for making 1 chair cover.

YARDAGE REQUIREMENTS
Yardage is based on 45"w fabric.

🟦 3/8 yd of green plaid

🟥 1/8 yd of red print

⬜ 1/8 yd of tan plaid

⬛ assorted scraps for appliqués
7/8 yd of green plaid for backing and binding
16" x 35" batting

You will also need:
transparent monofilament thread for appliqué
paper-backed fusible web
8 assorted black buttons

CUTTING OUT THE PIECES
All measurements include a ¼" seam allowance. Follow Rotary Cutting, page 144, to cut fabric unless otherwise indicated.

1. **From green plaid:**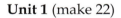
   - Cut 1 **background** 11½" x 26½".
2. **From red print:**
   - Cut 1 **strip** 1½"w.
3. **From tan plaid:**
   - Cut 1 **strip** 1½"w.
4. **From assorted scraps:**
   - Use patterns and follow Steps 1 - 3 of **Invisible Appliqué**, page 148, to cut out 1 **appliqué** from each pattern.

ASSEMBLING THE CHAIR COVER
Follow Piecing and Pressing, page 146, to make chair cover.

1. Fold **background** in half with short ends together; press. Referring to **Chair Cover Diagram**, follow Steps 4 - 14 of **Invisible Appliqué**, page 149, to center and stitch **appliqués** to each half of **background**.
2. Sew **strips** together to make **Strip Set**. Cut across **Strip Set** at 1½" intervals to make 22 **Unit 1's**.

Strip Set (make 1)   **Unit 1** (make 22)

1½"

3. Sew 11 **Unit 1's** together to make **Pieced Border**. Make 2 **Pieced Borders**.

Pieced Border (make 2)

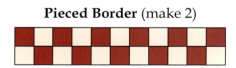

4. Refer to **Chair Cover Diagram** to sew **Pieced Borders** to **background** to complete top of **Chair Cover**.

COMPLETING THE CHAIR COVER
1. Cut 1 backing piece 16" x 35". Follow **Quilting**, page 151, to mark, layer, and quilt. Our chair cover is hand quilted in the ditch around appliqués and along seamlines.
2. Trim batting and backing even with edges of chair cover top. Cut 2 strips 2½" x 30½" and 2 strips 2½" x 42" from binding fabric. Press strips in half lengthwise, wrong sides together.
3. Follow Steps 1 and 3 of **Attaching Binding with Overlapped Corners**, page 157, to attach 30½"l binding strips to long edges of chair cover.
4. Matching raw edges, center 42"l strips on short edges of chair cover top, leaving excess binding to form ties; sew in place using ¼" seam allowance. Fold binding over to backing, finger pressing ties so that raw edges are enclosed in binding; pin in place. Blindstitch binding in place.
5. Knot ends of ties. Sew on buttons.

Chair Cover Diagram

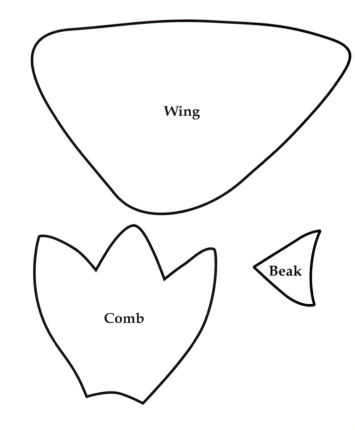

Wing

Comb

Beak

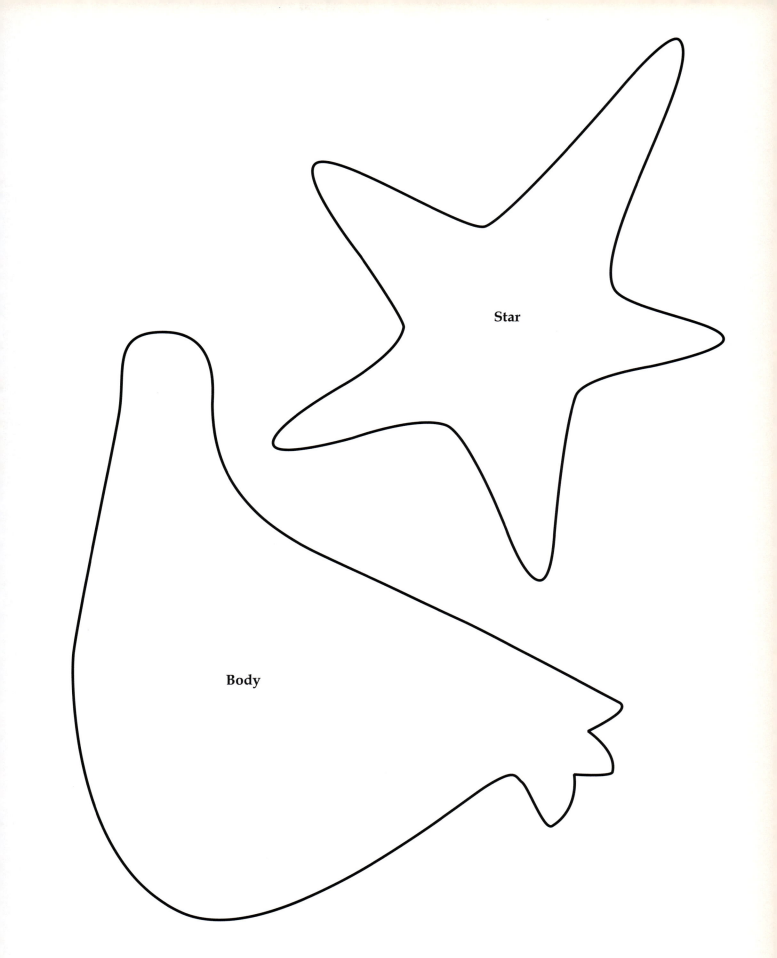

Star

Body

ROMAN STRIPE

Known as Roman Stripe when pieced using print fabrics, this classic pattern is more commonly called Sunshine and Shadows among the Amish of the Midwest. Quilters in these communities traditionally use only solid fabrics for the stripes with black as the background. For our Roman Stripe quilt, we selected a variety of rustic plaids for a homespun look, but almost any color combination works well — using black for the solid triangles helps blend the tones beautifully! To create the striped sections, we rotary cut strip-pieced sets using a special ruler that produces accurate angles with ease. The fast and simple pattern, completed with basic borders, is a delightful project for any first-time quilter.

ROMAN STRIPE QUILT

SKILL LEVEL: 1 2 3 4 5
BLOCK SIZE: 7" x 7"
QUILT SIZE: 78" x 92"

YARDAGE REQUIREMENTS

Yardage is based on 45"w fabric.

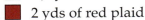

- $4^5/8$ yds of black plaid
- $2^3/4$ yds **total** of assorted plaids
- 2 yds of red plaid
- $1^7/8$ yds of black solid
  $7^1/4$ yds for backing
  1 yd for binding
  90" x 108" batting

You will also need:
Companion Angle™ Rotary Cutting Ruler (made by EZ International)

CUTTING OUT THE PIECES

All measurements include a ¼" seam allowance. Follow Rotary Cutting, page 144, to cut fabric.

1. **From black plaid:** ■
   - Cut 2 lengthwise strips $12^1/4$" x 82" for **top/bottom outer borders**.
   - Cut 2 lengthwise strips $12^1/4$" x 72" for **side outer borders**.

2. **From assorted plaids:** ◩
   - Cut a total of 44 **strips** $1^3/4$"w.

3. **From red plaid:** ■
   - Cut 2 lengthwise strips $2^3/4$" x 67" for **side inner borders**.
   - Cut 2 lengthwise strips $2^3/4$" x 58" for **top/bottom inner borders**.

4. **From black solid:** ■
   - Cut 7 strips $7^7/8$"w. From these strips, cut 32 squares $7^7/8$" x $7^7/8$". Cut squares once diagonally to make 64 **triangles** (you will need 63 and have 1 left over).

square (cut 32)

$7^7/8$"
$7^7/8$"

triangle (cut 64)

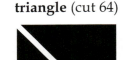

ASSEMBLING THE QUILT TOP

*Follow **Piecing and Pressing**, page 146, to make quilt top.*

1. Sew 4 **strips** together in random color order to make **Strip Set**. Make 11 **Strip Sets**.

Strip Set (make 11)

2. Aligning top and bottom edges of ruler with long edges of strip set, use Companion Angle ruler to cut 63 **Unit 1's** from **Strip Sets**, turning ruler 180° after each cut (**Fig. 1**).

Fig. 1

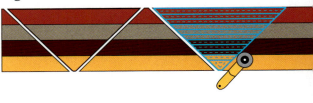

Unit 1 (make 63)

3. Sew 1 **Unit 1** and 1 **triangle** together to make **Block**. Make 63 **Blocks**.

Block (make 63)

4. Sew 7 **Blocks** together to make **Row**. Make 9 **Rows**.

Row (make 9)

Referring to **Quilt Top Diagram**, sew **Rows** together to make center section of quilt top. Follow **Adding Squared Borders**, page 150, to sew **side**, then **top** and **bottom inner borders** to center section. Add **side**, then **top** and **bottom outer borders** to complete **Quilt Top**.

COMPLETING THE QUILT

Follow **Quilting**, page 151, to mark, layer, and quilt, using **Quilting Diagram** as a suggestion. Our quilt is machine quilted.

Cut a 34" square of binding fabric. Follow **Binding**, page 155, to bind quilt using 2 1/2"w bias binding with mitered corners.

Quilting Diagram

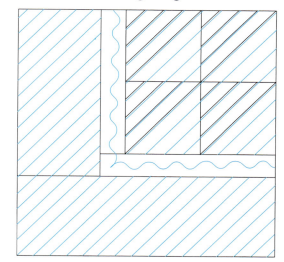

Quilt Top Diagram

QUILTER'S CHRISTMAS COLLECTION

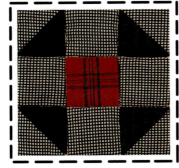

In pioneer homes, quilters used their creative talents to celebrate the holiday season. Guests were welcomed by quaint decorations handcrafted from fabric scraps and stray buttons. Today we can recapture that charm with the ideas found in our Quilter's Christmas Collection. For our wonderful wall hanging, we used a variety of fast techniques, including a grid method for creating the triangle-squares and fast machine appliqué using clear nylon thread. Finished with fused-on shapes and permanent-pen "stitches," our heartfelt sentiments will spread wishes of "piece" and joy to all your Yuletide guests!

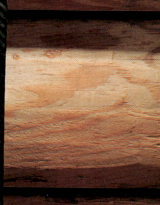

Hung with care, our appliquéd stockings (opposite) will hold Santa's best surprises! We used paper-backed fusible web and clear nylon thread for the evergreen and heart appliqués. Creating the prairie points is a snap — just fold fabric squares and then stitch them in place. A vintage suit vest (left) becomes a palette for expressing your love of quilting. Choose your favorite appliqués and pieced blocks from this section to create a one-of-a-kind gift any Santa's helper would appreciate. Complete your holiday decor with these seasonal throw pillows (below). The welted cushion boasts a cheerful Kris Kringle appliqué, and our Shoo Fly pillowcase will dress up any pillow.

QUILTER'S CHRISTMAS WALL HANGING

SKILL LEVEL: 1 2 3 4 5
WALL HANGING SIZE: 27" x 28"

YARDAGE REQUIREMENTS
Yardage is based on 45"w fabric.

 ½ yd of green check

1 fat quarter (18" x 22" piece) **each** of cream plaid, tan print, 3 red plaids, tan check, brown check, 2 gold prints, and 4 green prints

scraps of cream solid, cream check, dark brown print, white print, and black solid for appliqués
3" x 7" rectangle of white print for mini quilts
1 yd for backing and hanging sleeve
½ yd for binding
31" x 31" batting
3" x 7" rectangle of batting for mini quilts

You will also need:
transparent monofilament thread for appliqué
paper-backed fusible web
black and pink permanent fabric markers
12" of jute twine

CUTTING OUT THE PIECES
All measurements include a ¼" seam allowance. Follow **Rotary Cutting**, *page 144, to cut fabric.*

1. **From green check:**
   - Cut 2 **top/bottom borders** 3½" x 21½".
   - Cut 2 **side borders** 3½" x 21".
   - Cut 1 **rectangle** 5" x 9" for triangle-squares.

2. **From cream plaid:**
   - Cut 1 **medium rectangle** 3½" x 6".
   - Cut 3 **large squares** 3½" x 3½".

3. **From tan print:**
   - Cut 1 **rectangle** 5" x 9" for triangle-squares.
   - Cut 16 **small squares** 1½" x 1½".
   - Cut 1 **large rectangle** 6½" x 8½".
   - Cut 3 **medium squares** 3" x 3".

4. **From red plaids:**
   - Cut 1 **strip** 2" x 22".
   - Cut 4 **border corner squares** 3½" x 3½".
   - Cut a total of 3 **squares** 3½" x 3½" from 2 plaids.
   - Cut 3 **small squares** 1½" x 1½".
   - Cut 1 **long rectangle** 1½" x 12½".
   - Cut 1 **medium rectangle** 1½" x 6½".
   - Cut 1 **small rectangle** 1" x 3".

5. **From tan check:**
   - Cut 1 **background** 11½" x 12½".

6. **From brown check:**
   - Cut 1 **rectangle** 5" x 9" for triangle-squares.
   - Cut 12 **small squares** 1½" x 1½".
   - Cut 4 **medium squares** 3" x 3".

7. **From 1 gold print:**
   - Cut 1 **rectangle** 5" x 9" for triangle-squares.
   - Cut 4 **small squares** 1½" x 1½".

8. **From 1 green print:**
   - Cut 1 **strip** 2" x 22".

CUTTING OUT THE APPLIQUÉS
Use patterns, pages 138 - 139, and follow Steps 1 - 3 of **Invisible Appliqué**, *page 148, to cut appliqués.*

1. **From tan print:**
   - Cut 2 **Cuffs** (1 in reverse).
   - Cut 1 **Cap Trim**.
   - Cut 1 **Coat Trim**.

2. **From red plaids:**
   - Cut 4 **Small Hearts**.
   - Cut 1 **Coat**.
   - Cut 1 **Cap**.

3. **From gold prints:**
   - Cut 3 **Large Hearts**.
   - Cut 4 **Large Stars**.
   - Cut 5 **Small Stars**.

4. **From green prints:**
   - Cut 1 **Large Tree**.
   - Cut 2 **Medium Trees**.
   - Cut 3 **Small Trees**.
   - Cut 1 **Grass**.

5. **From cream solid:**
   - Cut 1 **Face**.

6. **From cream check:**
   - Cut 3 **Small Hearts**.

7. **From dark brown print:**
   - Cut 3 **Tree Trunks**.

8. **From white print:**
   - Cut 1 **Beard**.
   - Cut 1 **Mustache**.

9. **From black solid:**
   - Cut 2 **Gloves** (1 in reverse).
   - Cut 2 **Boots** (1 in reverse).

ASSEMBLING THE WALL HANGING TOP
Follow **Piecing and Pressing**, *page 146, to make wall hanging top.*

1. To make triangle-squares, place green check and brown check **rectangles** right sides together. Referring to **Fig. 1**, follow **Making Triangle-Squares**, page 147, to make a total of 16 **triangle-squares** (you will need 12 and have 4 left over).

Fig. 1   triangle-square (make 16)

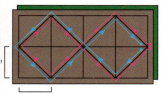

1⅞"

Sew 4 **triangle-squares** and 5 **small squares** together to make **Shoo Fly Block**. Make 3 **Shoo Fly Blocks**.

Shoo Fly Block (make 3)

Using tan print and gold print **rectangles**, repeat Step 1 to make 16 **triangle-squares**.
Sew 4 **triangle-squares** and 5 **small squares** together to make **Friendship Star Block**. Make 4 **Friendship Star Blocks**.

Friendship Star Block (make 4)

Sew **strips** together to make 1 **Strip Set**. Cut across **Strip Set** at 3½" intervals to make 6 **Red/Green Blocks**.

Strip Set (make 1)   **Red/Green Block** (make 6)

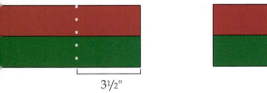

3½"

Sew **background** and **long rectangle** together. (*Note:* For Steps 7 - 12, refer to photo and **Assembly Diagram**, page 134, and follow Steps 4 - 14 of **Invisible Appliqué**, page 149.) Stitch **Grass**, Santa appliqué pieces, 1 **Medium Tree**, 1 **Tree Trunk** (trimmed to 1¼"l), and **Small Stars** to **background**. Use markers to draw eyes and nose on **Face** and "stitches" on **Beard** and **Mustache** to complete **Santa Block**.

Santa Block

8. Stitch **Large Tree** and **Tree Trunk** to **large rectangle**.
9. Stitch 1 **Medium Tree** and 1 **Tree Trunk** (trimmed to 2¼"l) to **medium rectangle**.
10. Stitch **Large Hearts**, then cream print **Small Hearts** to 3 red plaid **squares**. Use black marker to write "Joy," "Piece," and "Quilt" and to draw "stitches" on **Small Hearts**.
11. Stitch red plaid **Small Hearts** and **Small Trees** to **medium squares**.
12. Stitch **Large Stars** to **border corner squares**.
13. Referring to **Assembly Diagram**, page 134, sew 2 **Red/Green Blocks**, **large rectangle**, red plaid **medium rectangle**, and then **Santa Block** together to make **Unit 1**. Sew red plaid **small rectangle** and **medium squares** together to make **Unit 2**. Sew cream plaid **medium rectangle** and red plaid **squares** together to make **Unit 3**. Sew **Friendship Star Blocks**, **Red/Green Blocks**, **Shoo Fly Blocks**, and **large squares** together to make **Unit 4**.
14. Sew **Units** together in numerical order to make center section of wall hanging top.
15. Sew 1 **border corner square** to each end of **top/bottom borders**. Sew **side**, then **top** and **bottom borders** to center section to complete **Wall Hanging Top**.

COMPLETING THE WALL HANGING

1. Follow **Quilting**, page 151, to mark, layer, and quilt, using **Quilting Diagram**, page 134, as a suggestion. Our wall hanging is machine quilted.
2. Follow **Making a Hanging Sleeve**, page 157, to attach hanging sleeve to wall hanging.
3. Cut a 16" square of binding fabric. Follow **Binding**, page 155, to bind wall hanging using 2"w bias binding with mitered corners.
4. To make mini-quilts clothesline, use web to fuse white print rectangle to batting rectangle. Cut out 3 squares 2" x 2". Use patterns, page 137, and follow Steps 1 - 4 of **Invisible Appliqué**, page 148, to cut and fuse mini-quilt appliqués to squares. Use marker to add "stitches." Tack mini quilts to jute twine. Tack ends of twine to Santa's gloves.

Assembly Diagram

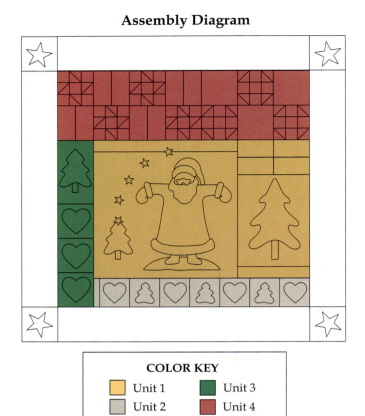

COLOR KEY

▮	Unit 1	▮	Unit 3
▮	Unit 2	▮	Unit 4

Quilting Diagram

KRIS KRINGLE PILLOW

PILLOW SIZE: 17" x 18"

SUPPLIES

11" x 12" piece of fabric for **background**
4 strips of fabric 1¼" x 13½" for **inner borders**
4 strips of fabric 2¾" x 17½" for **outer borders**
18" x 19" piece of fabric for **pillow back**
scraps of assorted fabrics for appliqués
2¼ yds of 3"w bias strip for welting
2¼ yds of ½" cord for welting
paper-backed fusible web
transparent monofilament thread for appliqué
red, green, pink, and black permanent fabric
   markers
polyester fiberfill

MAKING THE PILLOW

*Refer to photo and follow **Piecing and Pressing**, page 146 to make pillow top.*

1. Use patterns, pages 138 - 140, and follow
   Steps 1 - 3 of **Invisible Appliqué**, page 148,
   to cut the following appliqué pieces:

1 **Face**	2 **Gloves** (1 in reverse)
1 **Beard**	2 **Boots** (1 in reverse)
1 **Mustache**	2 **Medium Trees**
1 **Coat**	2 **Tree Trunks**
1 **Coat Trim**	1 **Grass**
2 **Cuffs** (1 in reverse)	1 **Banner**
1 **Cap**	2 **Large Stars**
1 **Cap Trim**	4 **Small Stars**

2. Follow Steps 4 - 14 of **Invisible Appliqué**,
   page 149, to stitch **appliqués** to **background**.
3. Use markers to write "Merry Christmas" and to
   draw holly leaves, berries, and border design on
   Banner; draw "stitches" on **Beard** and **Mustache**
   and eyes and nose on **Face**.
4. Sew **top**, **bottom**, then **side inner borders** to
   background, trimming off remainder of each
   strip after stitching. Repeat to add **outer borders**.
5. Follow Steps 4 - 14 of **Invisible Appliqué**,
   page 149, to stitch **Large Stars** to **outer borders**
   at opposite corners to complete **Pillow Top**.
6. Follow **Pillow Finishing**, page 158, to complete
   pillow with welting.

SHOO FLY PILLOW CASE

PILLOW CASE SIZE: 14" x 17"

YARDAGE REQUIREMENTS

Yardage is based on 45"w fabric.

- 3/4 yd of green check
- 1/4 yd of tan print
- 1/8 yd of red plaid

You will also need:
- covered button kit for three 1" buttons
- 14" x 14" pillow form

CUTTING OUT THE PIECES

All measurements include a 1/4" seam allowance. Follow Rotary Cutting, page 144, to cut fabric.

- **From green check:**
  - Cut 1 pillow case **back** 15 1/2" x 18 1/2".
  - Cut 1 **rectangle** 5" x 11" for triangle-squares.
  - Cut 2 **side outer borders** 4" x 11 1/2".
  - Cut 2 **top/bottom outer borders** 2 1/2" x 18 1/2".
  - Cut 2 **facings** 3" x 15 1/2".

- **From tan print:**
  - Cut 1 **rectangle** 5" x 11" for triangle-squares.
  - Cut 1 strip 1 1/2"w. From this strip, cut 20 **small squares** 1 1/2" x 1 1/2".
  - Cut 4 **large squares** 3 1/2" x 3 1/2".

- **From red plaid:**
  - Cut 2 **top/bottom inner borders** 1 1/2" x 9 1/2".
  - Cut 2 **side inner borders** 1 1/2" x 11 1/2".
  - Cut 5 **small squares** 1 1/2" x 1 1/2".

MAKING THE PILLOW CASE

Follow Piecing and Pressing, page 146, to make pillow case.

1. To make triangle-squares, place green check and tan print **rectangles** right sides together. Referring to **Fig. 1**, follow **Making Triangle-Squares**, page 147, to make a total of 20 **triangle-squares**.

Fig. 1

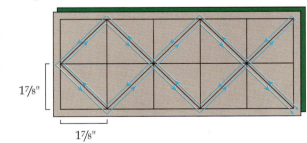

triangle-square (make 20)

2. Sew 4 **triangle-squares** and 5 **small squares** together to make **Block**. Make 5 **Blocks**.

Block (make 5)

3. Referring to photo, sew 5 **Blocks** and 4 **large squares** together to make center section of pillow case top.
4. Sew **top**, **bottom**, then **side inner borders** to center section. Add **side**, then **top** and **bottom outer borders** to complete **Pillow Case Top**.
5. Stitch **Pillow Case Top** and **back** together leaving 1 side open; turn right side out.
6. Stitch short edges of **facings** together to form a loop. Press 1 raw edge 1/4" to wrong side and stitch in place. Aligning seams and matching right sides and raw edges, place facing over open end of pillow case; stitch together along raw edges. Press facing to inside of pillow case.
7. Referring to photo, work 3 evenly-spaced buttonholes 1" from edge of pillow case top.
8. Follow manufacturer's instructions to cover buttons with red plaid. Sew buttons to inside of pillow case back to complete **Pillow Case**.
9. Insert pillow form; button to close.

CHRISTMAS STOCKINGS

Instructions are for making 1 stocking.

SUPPLIES

- 2 pieces of cream print fabric 12" x 20" for stocking
- 2 pieces of fabric 12" x 20" for stocking lining
- 1 piece of cream plaid fabric 3" x 16" for cuff
- 2 pieces of red plaid fabric 1 1/2" x 16" for cuff borders
- 1 piece of fabric 5" x 16" for cuff lining
- 1 piece of fabric 2" x 8" for hanger
- 6 squares 4" x 4" of green check fabric for prairie points
- 2 squares 5" x 5" of red plaid fabric for heel and toe appliqués
- scraps of red or green fabric for cuff appliqués
- paper-backed fusible web
- transparent monofilament thread for appliqué
- tracing paper

MAKING THE STOCKING

*Follow **Piecing and Pressing**, page 146, to make stocking.*

1. Matching registration marks (⊕) and overlapping pattern pieces, trace **Stocking** pattern, page 141, onto tracing paper. Draw a second line 1/4" outside the first line; cut out pattern along outer line.

2. Place stocking fabric pieces right sides together and use pattern to cut out 2 stocking pieces; repeat for lining pieces.

3. Using red plaid squares and patterns, page 140, follow **Invisible Appliqué**, page 148, to stitch 1 **Heel** and 1 **Toe** to stocking front piece.

4. Sew stocking pieces together, leaving top open. Clip seam allowance at curves and turn right side out. Sew lining pieces together; do not turn.

5. Place lining inside stocking, matching seams and raw edges; baste raw edges together. Set stocking aside.

6. (*Note:* Refer to photo and **Fig. 1** for Steps 6 and 7.) Sew cuff and cuff border pieces together. Using scrap fabrics and patterns, page 139, follow **Invisible Appliqué**, page 148, to stitch 3 **Small Hearts** or 3 **Small Trees** to cuff.

7. To make prairie points, fold each square in half diagonally with wrong sides together; fold in half again and press (see **Fig. 2**, page 137). Baste prairie points to cuff, overlapping as necessary.

Fig. 1

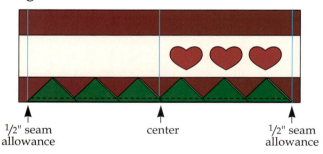

|← 1/2" seam allowance | ↑ center | ↑ 1/2" seam allowance |

8. Sew cuff and cuff lining together along lower edge, enclosing raw edges of prairie points in seam. Open and press. Fold cuff in half, matching right sides and short edges. Using a 1/2" seam allowance, sew short edges together to form a tube; turn right side out. To fold cuff in half, fold bottom raw edge of lining to inside to meet top raw edge of cuff; press.

9. For hanger, press long edges of 2" x 8" fabric piece 1/2" to wrong side. With wrong sides together, press in half lengthwise; stitch close to pressed edges. Fold hanger in half to form a loop. Matching raw edges of loop to raw edges of stocking at heel side seamline, pin hanger in place inside stocking.

10. To attach cuff to stocking, place cuff inside stocking with right side of cuff facing inside of stocking. With seamline of cuff matching heel side seamline of stocking, match raw edges and sew cuff and stocking together. Fold cuff down over stocking.

HOLIDAY VEST

Our instructions provide general guidelines for piecing the rectangles of fabric to cover vest fronts. We encourage you to use different appliqués or leftover pieced blocks from other projects to create your own special design.

SUPPLIES

a men's suit vest (we found ours at a resale shop)
1 yd of background fabric for vest fronts
1/4 yd of fabric for prairie points
fat quarters (18" x 22" pieces of fabric) and scraps of assorted fabrics in desired colors for pieced areas and appliqués
paper-backed fusible web
transparent monofilament thread for appliqué
assorted buttons
tracing paper

MAKING THE VEST

1. Remove buttons from vest. Use seam ripper to take vest apart at shoulder and side seams. Set aside vest back.

2. To make pattern, place right vest front piece, right side up, on tracing paper. Use a pencil to draw around vest front piece; draw a second line 1/4" outside the first. Cut out along outer line and label pattern. Repeat for left vest front piece.

3. To cover vest fronts, follow **Piecing and Pressing**, page 146, to piece a rectangle large enough for **each** pattern piece (**Fig. 1**). Our rectangles were pieced using **Shoo Fly Blocks** (follow Steps 1 and 2 of **Assembling the Wall Hanging Top**, page 132, to make 3 **Blocks**; we used 2 and had 1 left over), pieced strips made with 2" red and green squares, and 1 1/2"w strips of red plaid.

Fig. 1

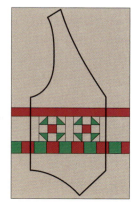

Place pattern pieces, right side down, on wrong side of pieced rectangles; cut out.

Use desired patterns, pages 138 - 139, and follow **Invisible Appliqué**, page 148, to stitch appliqués to vest fronts.

To make prairie points, cut desired number of 4" x 4" fabric squares. Fold each square in half diagonally with wrong sides together; fold in half again and press (**Fig. 2**). Referring to **Fig. 3**, arrange prairie points along front edges of **original** vest fronts with raw edges of points overlapping vest edge ½"; baste in place.

Fig. 2

Fig. 3

To make patterns for web, draw a third line ¼" inside first line on tracing paper patterns. Cut out along innermost line. Place patterns, right

side down, on paper backing side of web. Draw around each pattern and cut out. Center 1 web shape on wrong side of each pieced vest front; fuse in place. Remove paper backing.

8. For each vest front, center pieced vest front, right side up, on right side of original vest front (fabric will extend past vest edges ¼"); fuse in place.

9. Press raw edges of each pieced vest front under ¼" so that pressed edges match edges of original vest fronts. Topstitch in place through all layers.

10. To reassemble vest, refer to **Fig. 4** and insert shoulder and side seam allowances of vest front pieces between lining and outer fabric of vest back at shoulder and side seams. Topstitch through all layers.

Fig. 4

11. Fold prairie points to right side of vest front and sew a button through each to secure. Sew on other buttons as desired.

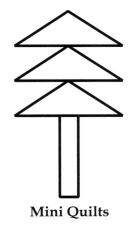

Mini Quilts

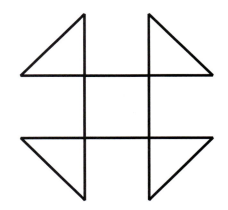

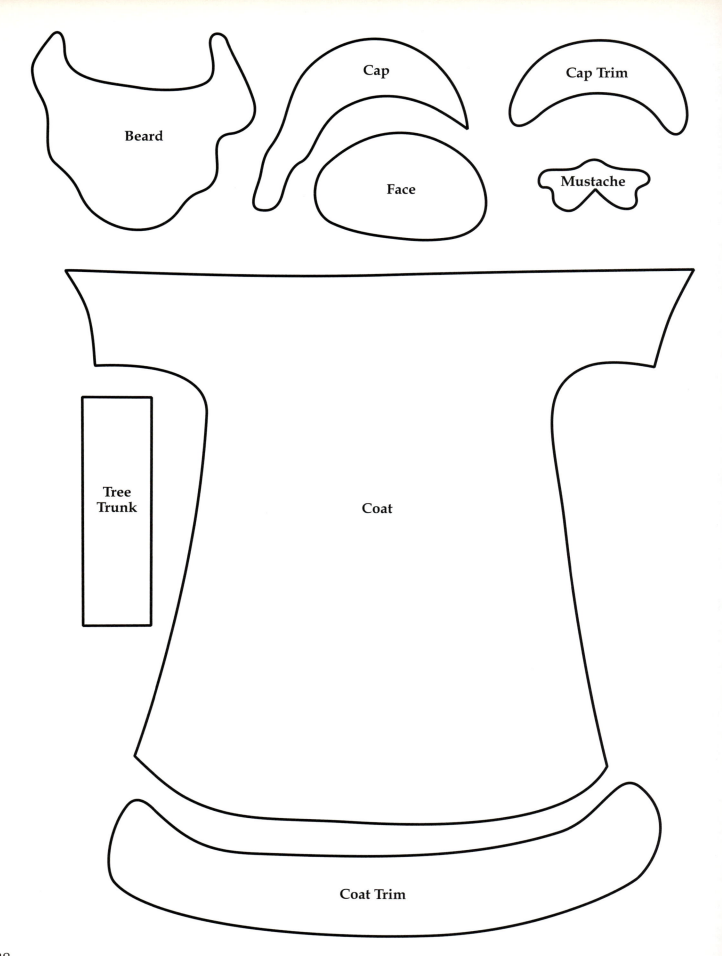

Beard

Cap

Cap Trim

Face

Mustache

Tree
Trunk

Coat

Coat Trim

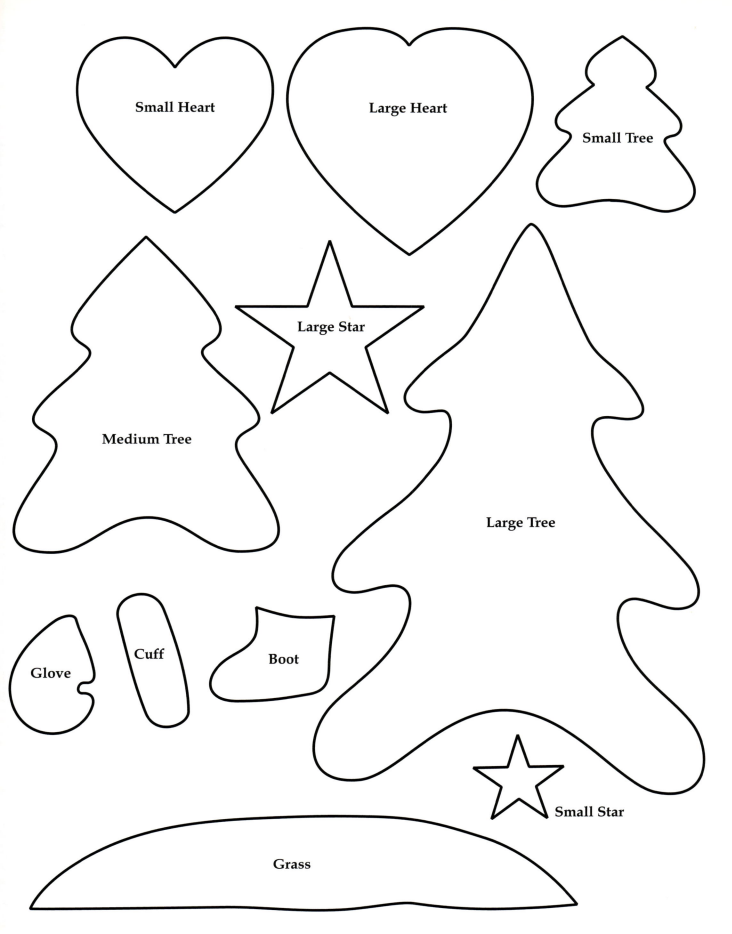

Small Heart

Large Heart

Small Tree

Medium Tree

Large Star

Large Tree

Glove

Cuff

Boot

Small Star

Grass

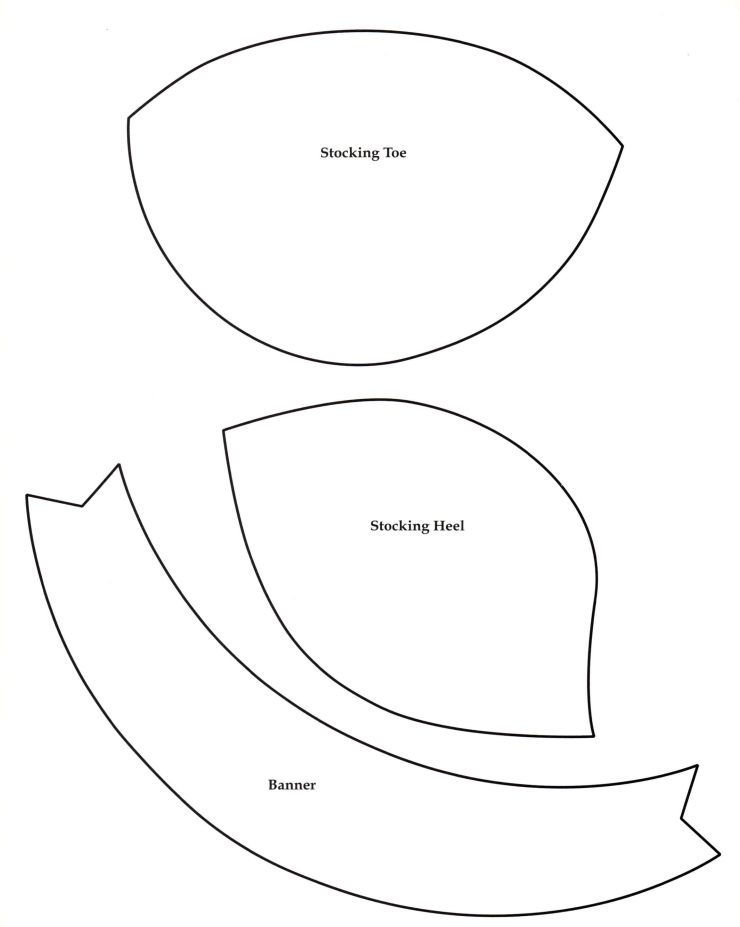

Stocking Toe

Stocking Heel

Banner

140

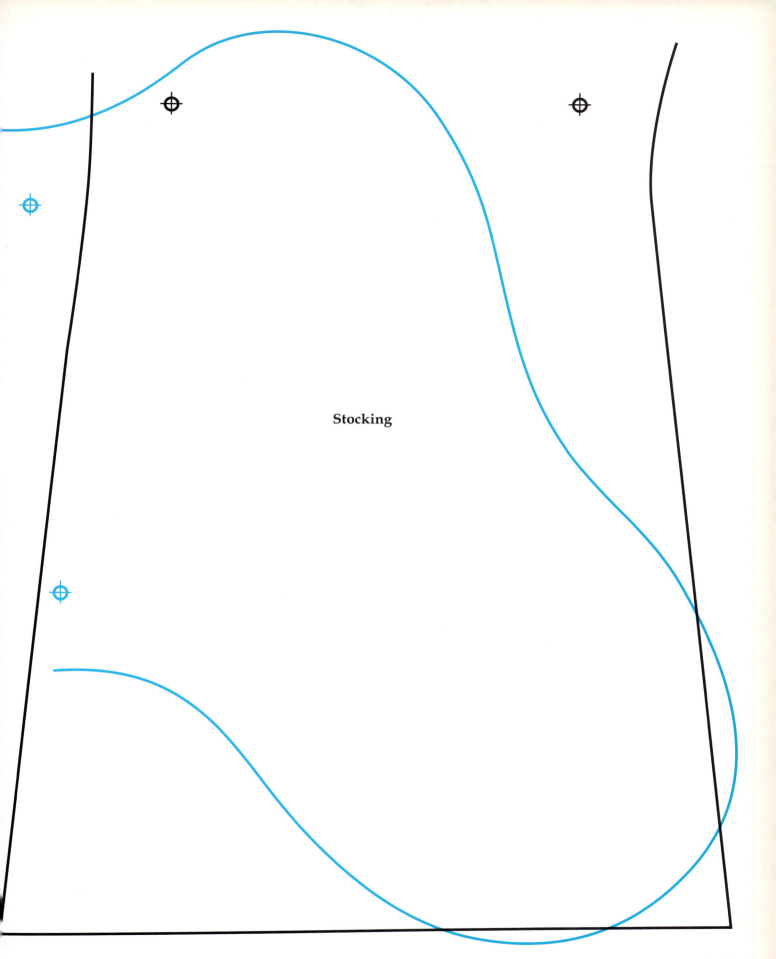

Stocking

GENERAL INSTRUCTIONS

Complete instructions are given for making each of the quilts and accompanying projects shown in this book. Skill levels indicated for quilts and wall hangings may help you choose the right project. To make your quilting easier and more enjoyable, we encourage you to carefully read all of these general instructions, study the color photographs, and familiarize yourself with the individual project instructions before beginning a project.

QUILTING SUPPLIES

This list includes all the tools you need for basic quick-method quiltmaking, plus additional supplies used for special techniques. Unless otherwise specified, all items may be found in your favorite fabric store or quilt shop.

Batting — Batting is most commonly available in polyester, cotton, or a cotton/polyester blend (see **Choosing and Preparing the Batting**, page 153).

Cutting mat — A cutting mat is a special mat designed to be used with a rotary cutter. A mat that measures approximately 18" x 24" is a good size for most cutting.

Eraser — A soft white fabric eraser or white art eraser may be used to remove pencil marks from fabric. Do not use a colored eraser, as the dye may discolor fabric.

Iron — An iron with both steam and dry settings and a smooth, clean soleplate is necessary for proper pressing.

Marking tools — There are many different types of marking tools available (see **Marking Quilting Lines**, page 152). A silver quilter's pencil is a good marker for both light and dark fabrics.

Masking Tape — Two widths of masking tape, 1"w and ¼"w, are helpful to have when quilting. The 1"w tape is used to secure the backing fabric to a flat surface when layering the quilt. The ¼"w tape may be used as a guide when outline quilting.

Needles — Two types of needles are used for hand sewing: *Betweens*, used for quilting, are short and strong for stitching through layered fabric and batting. *Sharps* are longer, thinner needles used for basting and other hand sewing. For *sewing machine needles*, we recommend size 10 to 14 or 70 to 90 universal (sharp-pointed) needles.

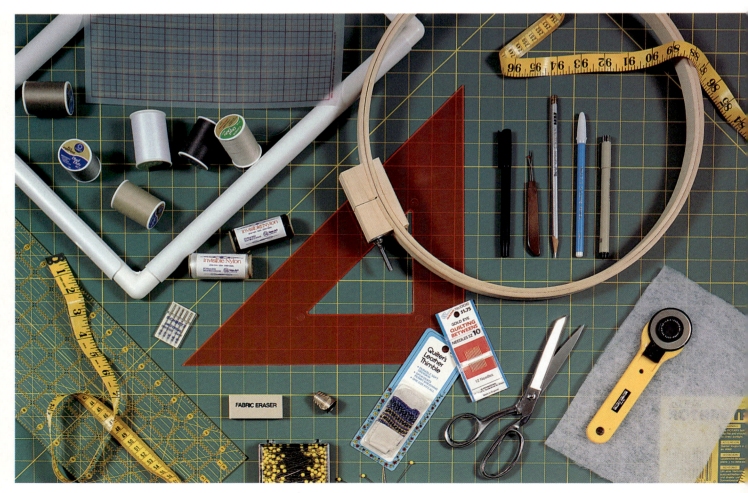

aper-backed fusible web — This iron-on adhesive with paper backing is used to secure fabric cutouts to another fabric when appliquéing. If the cutouts will be stitched in place, purchase the lighter weight web that will not gum up your sewing machine. A heavier weight web is used for appliqués that are fused in place with no additional stitching.

ermanent fine-point marker — A permanent marker is used to mark templates and stencils and to sign and date quilts. Test marker on fabric to make sure it will not bleed or wash out.

ns — Straight pins made especially for quilting are extra long with large, round heads. Glass head pins will stand up to occasional contact with a hot iron. Some quilters prefer extra-fine dressmaker's silk pins. If you are machine quilting, you will need a large supply of 1" long (size 01) rust-proof safety pins for pin-basting.

uilting hoop or frame — Quilting hoops and frames are designed to securely hold the 3 layers of a quilt together while you quilt. Many different types and sizes are available, including round and oval wooden hoops, frames made of rigid plastic pipe, and large floor frames made of either material. A 14" or 16" hoop allows you to quilt in your lap and makes your quilting portable.

otary cutter — The rotary cutter is the essential tool for quick-method quilting techniques. The cutter consists of a round, sharp blade mounted on a handle with a retractable blade guard for safety. It should be used only with a cutting mat and rotary cutting ruler. Two sizes are generally available; we recommend the larger (45 mm) size.

otary cutting rulers — A rotary cutting ruler is a thick, clear acrylic ruler made specifically for use with a rotary cutter. It should have accurate 1/8" crosswise and lengthwise markings and markings for 45° and 60° angles. A 6" x 24" ruler is a good size for most cutting. An additional 6" x 12" ruler or 12 1/2" square ruler is helpful when cutting wider pieces. Many specialty rulers are available that make specific cutting tasks faster and easier.

issors — Although most cutting will be done with a rotary cutter, sharp, high-quality scissors are still needed for some cutting. A separate pair of scissors for cutting paper and plastic is recommended. Smaller scissors are handy for clipping threads.

am ripper — A good seam ripper with a fine point is useful for removing stitching.

wing machine — A sewing machine that produces a good, even straight stitch is all that is necessary for most quilting. Zigzag stitch capability is necessary for Invisible Appliqué. Blindstitch with variable stitch width capability is required for Mock Hand Appliqué. Clean and oil your machine often and keep the tension set properly.

Stabilizer — Commercially made non-woven material or paper stabilizer is placed behind background fabric when doing Invisible Appliqué to provide a more stable stitching surface.

Tape measure — A flexible 120" long tape measure is helpful for measuring a quilt top before adding borders.

Template material — Sheets of translucent plastic, often pre-marked with a grid, are made especially for making templates and quilting stencils.

Thimble — A thimble is necessary when hand quilting. Thimbles are available in metal, plastic, or leather and in many sizes and styles. Choose a thimble that fits well and is comfortable.

Thread — Several types of thread are used for quiltmaking: *General-purpose* sewing thread is used for basting, piecing, and some appliquéing. Buy high-quality cotton or cotton-covered polyester thread in light and dark neutrals, such as ecru and grey, for your basic supplies. *Quilting* thread is stronger than general-purpose sewing thread, and some brands have a coating to make them slide more easily through the quilt layers. Some machine appliqué projects in this book use *transparent monofilament* (clear nylon) thread. Use a very fine (.004), soft nylon thread that is not stiff or wiry. Choose clear nylon thread for white or light fabrics or smoke nylon thread for darker fabrics.

Triangle — A large plastic right-angle triangle (available in art and office supply stores) is useful in rotary cutting for making first cuts to "square up" raw edges of fabric and for checking to see that cuts remain at right angles to the fold.

Walking foot — A walking foot or even-feed foot is needed for straight-line machine quilting. This special foot will help all 3 layers of the quilt move at the same rate over the feed dogs to provide a smoother quilted project.

FABRICS
SELECTING FABRICS

For many quilters, choosing fabrics for a new quilt project is one of the most fun, yet challenging, parts of quiltmaking. Photographs of our quilts are excellent guides for choosing the colors for your quilt. You may choose to duplicate the colors in the photograph, or you may use the same light, medium, and dark values in completely different color families. When you change the light and dark value placement in a quilt block, you may come up with a surprising new creation. The most important lesson to learn about fabrics and color is to choose fabrics you love. When you combine several fabrics you are simply crazy about in a quilt, you are sure to be happy with the results!

The yardage requirements listed for each project are based on 45" wide fabric with a "usable" width of 42" after shrinkage and trimming selvages. Your actual usable width will probably vary slightly from fabric to fabric. Though most fabrics will yield 42" or more, if you find a fabric that yields a narrower usable width you will need to purchase additional yardage to compensate. Our yardage lengths should be adequate for occasional resquaring of fabric when many cuts are required, but it never hurts to buy a little more fabric for insurance against a narrower usable width, the occasional cutting error, or to have on hand for making coordinating projects.

Choose high-quality, medium-weight, 100% cotton fabrics such as broadcloth or calico. All-cotton fabrics hold a crease better, fray less, and are easier to quilt than cotton/polyester blends. All the fabrics for a quilt should be of comparable weight and weave. Check the end of the fabric bolt for fiber content and width.

PREPARING FABRICS

All fabrics should be washed, dried, and pressed before cutting.

1. To check colorfastness before washing, cut a small piece of the fabric and place in a glass of hot water with a little detergent. Leave fabric in the water for a few minutes. Remove from water and blot fabric with white paper towels. If any color bleeds onto the towels, wash the fabric separately with warm water and detergent, then rinse until the water runs clear. If the fabric continues to bleed, choose another fabric.
2. Unfold yardage and separate fabrics by color. To help reduce raveling, use scissors to snip off a small triangle from each corner of your fabric pieces (**Fig. 1**). Machine wash fabrics in warm water with a small amount of mild laundry detergent. Do not use fabric softener. Rinse well and then dry fabrics in the dryer, checking long fabric lengths occasionally to make sure they are not tangling.

Fig. 1

3. To make ironing easier, remove fabrics from dryer while they are slightly damp. Refold each fabric lengthwise (as it was on the bolt) with wrong sides together and matching selvages. If necessary, adjust slightly at selvages so that the fold lies flat. Press each fabric with a steam iron set on "Cotton."

ROTARY CUTTING

*Based on the idea that you can easily cut strips of fabric and then cut those strips into smaller pieces, rotary cutting has brought speed and accuracy to quiltmaking. Observe safety precautions when using the rotary cutter since it is extremely sharp. Develop a habit of retracting the blade guard **just before** making a cut and closing it **immediately afterward**, before laying down the cutter.*

1. Follow **Preparing Fabrics** to wash, dry, and press fabrics.
2. Cut all strips from the selvage-to-selvage width of the fabric unless otherwise indicated. Place fabric on the cutting mat as shown in **Fig. 2** with the fold of the fabric toward you. To straighten the uneven fabric edge, make the first "squaring up" cut by placing the right edge of the rotary cutting ruler over the left raw edge of the fabric. Place right-angle triangle (or another rotary cutting ruler) with the lower edge carefully aligned with the fold and the left edge against the ruler (**Fig. 2**). Hold the ruler firmly with your left hand, placing your little finger off the left edge of the ruler to anchor it. Remove the triangle, pick up the rotary cutter, and retract the blade guard. Using a smooth, downward motion, make the cut by running the blade of the rotary cutter firmly along the right edge of the ruler (**Fig. 3**). **Always** cut in a direction **away** from your body and **immediately** close the blade guard after each cut.

Fig. 2

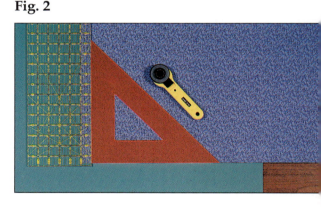

Fig. 3

After squaring up, cut the strips required for the project. Place the ruler over the cut edge of the fabric, aligning desired marking on the ruler with the cut edge (**Fig. 4**). When cutting several strips from a single piece of fabric, it is important to occasionally use the ruler and triangle to ensure that cuts are still at a perfect right angle to the fold. If not, repeat Step 2 to straighten.

Fig. 4

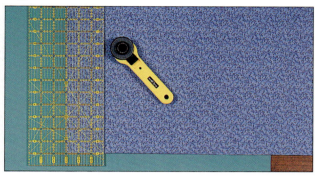

To square up selvage ends of a strip before cutting pieces, refer to **Fig. 5** and place folded strip on mat with selvage ends to your right. Aligning a horizontal marking on ruler with 1 long edge of strip, use rotary cutter to trim off selvage to make end of strip square and even (**Fig. 5**). Turn strip (or entire mat) so that cut end is to your left before making subsequent cuts.

Fig. 5

Pieces such as rectangles and squares can now be cut from strips. (Cutting other shapes like diamonds is discussed in individual project instructions.) Usually strips remain folded, and pieces are cut in pairs after ends of strips are squared up. To cut squares or rectangles from a strip, place ruler over left end of strip, aligning desired marking on ruler with cut end of strip. To ensure perfectly square cuts, align a horizontal marking on ruler with 1 long edge of strip (**Fig. 6**). Make cut as in Step 2.

Fig. 6

6. After some practice, you may want to try stacking up to 6 fabric layers when making cuts. When stacking strips, match long cut edges and follow Step 4 to square up ends of strip stack. Carefully turn stack (or entire mat) so that squared-up ends are at your left before making subsequent cuts. After cutting, check accuracy of pieces. Some shapes, such as diamonds, are more difficult to cut accurately in stacks.

7. In some cases, strips will be sewn together into strip sets before being cut into smaller units. When cutting a strip set, align a seam in the strip set with a horizontal marking on the ruler to maintain square cuts (**Fig. 7**). We do not recommend stacking strip sets for rotary cutting.

Fig. 7

8. Most borders for quilts in this book are cut along the more stable lengthwise grain to minimize wavy edges caused by stretching. To remove selvages before cutting lengthwise strips, place fabric on mat with selvages to your left and squared-up end at bottom of mat. Placing ruler over selvage and using squared-up edge instead of fold, follow Step 2 to cut away selvages as you did raw edges (**Fig. 8**). After making a cut the length of the mat, move the next section of fabric to be cut onto the mat. Repeat until you have removed selvages from required length of fabric.

Fig. 8

9. After removing selvages, place ruler over left edge of fabric, aligning desired marking on ruler with cut edge of fabric. Make cuts as in Step 3. After each cut, move next section of fabric onto mat as in Step 8.

TEMPLATE CUTTING

Our full-sized piecing templates have 2 lines: a solid cutting line and a dashed line showing the ¼" seam allowance.

1. To make a template from a pattern, use a permanent fine-point marker to carefully trace pattern onto template plastic, making sure to transfer all alignment and grain line markings. Cut out template along inner edge of drawn line. Check template against original pattern for accuracy.
2. To use a template, place template on wrong side of fabric (unless indicated otherwise), aligning grain line on template with straight grain of fabric. Use a sharp fabric marking pencil to draw around template. Transfer all alignment markings to fabric. Cut out fabric piece using scissors or rotary cutter and ruler.

PIECING AND PRESSING

Precise cutting, followed by accurate piecing and careful pressing, will ensure that all the pieces of your quilt top fit together well.

PIECING

Set sewing machine stitch length for approximately 11 stitches per inch. Use a new, sharp needle suited for medium-weight woven fabric.

Use a neutral-colored general-purpose sewing thread (not quilting thread) in the needle and in the bobbin. Stitch first on a scrap of fabric to check upper and bobbin thread tension and make any adjustments necessary.

For good results, it is **essential** that you stitch with an **accurate ¼" seam allowance**. On many sewing machines, the measurement from the needle to the outer edge of the presser foot is ¼". If this is the case with your machine, the presser foot is your best guide. If not, measure ¼" from the needle and mark with a piece of masking tape. Special presser feet that are exactly ¼" wide are also available for most sewing machines.

When piecing, **always** place pieces **right sides together** and **match raw edges**; pin if necessary. (If using straight pins, remove the pins just before they reach the sewing machine needle.)

Chain Piecing

Chain piecing whenever possible will make your work go faster and will usually result in more accurate piecing. Stack the pieces you will be sewing beside your machine in the order you will need them and in a position that will allow you to easily pick them up. Pick up each pair of pieces, carefully place them together as they will be sewn, and feed them into the machine one after the other. Stop between each pair only long enough to pick up the next and don't cut thread between pairs (**Fig. 9**). After all pieces are sewn, cut threads, press, and go on to the next step, chain piecing when possible.

Fig. 9

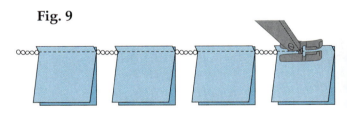

Sewing Strip Sets

When there are several strips to assemble into a strip set, first sew the strips together into pairs, then sew the pairs together to form the strip set. To help avoid distortion, sew 1 seam in 1 direction and then sew the next seam in the opposite direction (**Fig. 10**).

Fig. 10

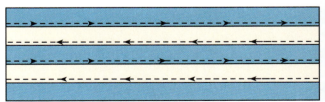

Sewing Across Seam Intersections

When sewing across the intersection of 2 seams, place pieces right sides together and match seams exactly, making sure seam allowances are pressed in opposite directions (**Fig. 11**). To prevent fabric from shifting, you may wish to pin in place.

Fig. 11

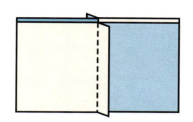

Sewing Sharp Points

To ensure sharp points when joining triangular or diagonal pieces, stitch across the center of the "X" (shown in pink) formed on the wrong side by previous seams (**Fig. 12**).

Fig. 12

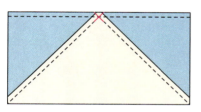

Sewing Bias Seams

Care should be used in handling and stitching bias edges, since they stretch easily. After sewing the seam, carefully press seam allowances to 1 side, making sure not to stretch the fabric.

Making Triangle-Squares

The grid method for making triangle-squares is faster and more accurate than cutting and sewing individual triangles. Stitching before cutting the triangle-squares apart also prevents stretching the bias edges.

Follow project instructions to cut rectangles or squares of fabric for making triangle-squares. Place the indicated pieces right sides together and press.
On the wrong side of the lighter fabric, draw a grid of squares similar to that shown in **Fig. 13**. The size and number of squares will be given in the project instructions.

Fig. 13

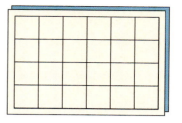

3. Following the example given in the project instructions, draw 1 diagonal line through each square in the grid (**Fig. 14**).

Fig. 14

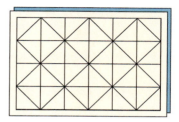

4. Stitch ¼" on each side of all diagonal lines. For accuracy, it may be helpful to first draw your stitching lines onto the fabric, especially if your presser foot is not your ¼" guide. In some cases, stitching may be done in a single continuous line. Project instructions include a diagram similar to **Fig. 15** which shows stitching lines and the direction of the stitching.

Fig. 15

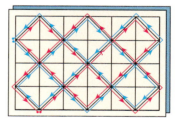

5. Use rotary cutter and ruler to cut along all drawn lines of the grid. Each square of the grid will yield 2 triangle-squares (**Fig. 16**).

Fig. 16

6. Carefully press triangle-squares open, pressing seam allowances toward darker fabric. Trim off points of seam allowances that extend beyond edges of triangle-square (see **Fig. 21**).

Working with Diamond Shapes

Piecing diamonds requires special handling. For best results, carefully follow the steps below to assemble the diamond sections of a block.

1. When sewing 2 diamond pieces together, place pieces right sides together, carefully matching edges; pin. Mark a small dot 1/4" from corner of 1 piece as shown in **Fig. 17**. Stitch pieces together in the direction shown, stopping at center of dot and backstitching.

Fig. 17

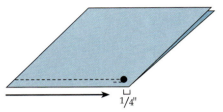

2. For best results, add side triangles, then corner squares to diamond sections. Mark corner of each piece to be set in with a small dot (**Fig. 18**).

3. To sew first seam, match right sides and pin the triangle or square to the diamond on the left. Stitch seam from the outer edge to the dot, backstitching at the dot; clip threads (**Fig. 19**).

Fig. 18

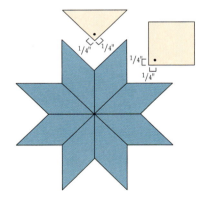

Fig. 19

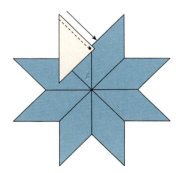

4. To sew the second seam, pivot the added triangle or square to match raw edges of next diamond. Beginning at dot, take 2 or 3 stitches, then backstitch, making sure not to backstitch into previous seam allowance. Continue stitching to outer edge (**Fig. 20**).

Fig. 20

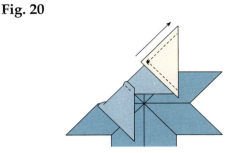

Trimming Seam Allowances

When sewing with diamond or triangle pieces, some seam allowances may extend beyond the edges of the sewn pieces. Trim away "dog ears" that extend beyond the edges of the sewn pieces (**Fig. 21**).

Fig. 21

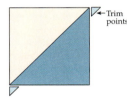

PRESSING

Use a steam iron set on "Cotton" for all pressing. Press as you sew, taking care to prevent small folds along seamlines. Seam allowances are almost always pressed to one side, usually toward the darker fabric. However, to reduce bulk it may occasionally be necessary to press seam allowances toward the lighter fabric or even to press them open. In order to prevent a dark fabric seam allowance from showing through a light fabric, trim the darker seam allowance slightly narrower than the lighter seam allowance.

APPLIQUÉ

INVISIBLE APPLIQUÉ

This method of machine appliqué is an adaptation of satin stitch appliqué that uses clear nylon thread to secure the appliqué pieces. Patterns are printed in reverse to enable you to use our speedy method of preparing appliqués.

1. Place paper-backed fusible web, web side down, over appliqué pattern. Use a pencil to trace pattern onto paper side of web as many times as indicated in project instructions for a single fabric. Repeat for additional patterns and fabric

Follow manufacturer's instructions to fuse traced patterns to wrong side of fabrics. Do not remove paper backing.

Use scissors to cut out appliqué pieces along traced lines. Remove paper backing from all pieces. Referring to diagram and/or photo, arrange appliqués on the background fabric and follow manufacturer's instructions to fuse in place. Pin a stabilizer, such as paper or any of the commercially available products, on wrong side of background fabric before stitching appliqués in place.

Thread sewing machine with transparent monofilament thread; use general-purpose thread that matches background fabric in bobbin. Set sewing machine for a very narrow (approximately 1/16") zigzag stitch and a short stitch length. You may find that loosening the top tension slightly will yield a smoother stitch. Begin by stitching 2 or 3 stitches in place (drop feed dogs or set stitch length at 0) to anchor thread. Most of the zigzag stitch should be done on the appliqué with the right edge of the stitch falling at the very outside edge of the appliqué (**Fig. 22**). Stitch over all exposed raw edges of appliqué pieces.

Fig. 22

(*Note:* Dots on **Figs. 23 - 28** indicate where to leave needle in fabric when pivoting.) For **outside corners**, stitch just past the corner, stopping with the needle in **background** fabric (**Fig. 23**). Raise presser foot. Pivot project, lower presser foot, and stitch adjacent side (**Fig. 24**).

Fig. 23   **Fig. 24**

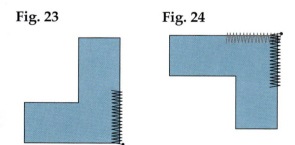

. For **inside corners**, stitch just past the corner, stopping with the needle in **appliqué** fabric (**Fig. 25**). Raise presser foot. Pivot project, lower presser foot, and stitch adjacent side (**Fig. 26**).

Fig. 25   **Fig. 26**

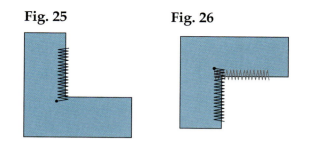

11. When stitching **outside** curves, stop with needle in **background** fabric. Raise presser foot and pivot project as needed. Lower presser foot and continue stitching, pivoting as often as necessary to follow curve (**Fig. 27**).

Fig. 27

12. When stitching **inside** curves, stop with needle in **appliqué** fabric. Raise presser foot and pivot project as needed. Lower presser foot and continue stitching, pivoting as often as necessary to follow curve (**Fig. 28**).

Fig. 28

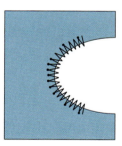

13. End stitching by sewing 2 or 3 stitches in place to anchor thread. Trim thread ends close to fabric.
14. Carefully tear away stabilizer.

MOCK HAND APPLIQUÉ

*This technique uses the blindstitch on your sewing machine to achieve a look that closely resembles traditional hand appliqué. Using an updated method, appliqués are prepared with turned under edges, and they are then machine stitched to the background fabric. For best results using Mock Hand Appliqué, your sewing machine must have blindstitch capability with a **variable** stitch width. If your blindstitch width cannot be adjusted, you may still wish to try this technique to see if you are happy with the results. Some sewing machines have a narrower blindstitch width than others.*

1. Follow project instructions to prepare appliqué pieces.
2. Thread needle of sewing machine with transparent monofilament thread; use general-purpose thread in bobbin in a color to match background fabric.
3. Set sewing machine for narrow blindstitch (just wide enough to catch 2 or 3 threads of the appliqué) and a very short stitch length (20 - 30 stitches per inch).
4. Arrange appliqué pieces on background fabric (or other appliqués) as described in project instructions. Use pins or hand baste to secure.
5. (*Note:* Follow Steps 9 - 12 of **Invisible Appliqué**, page 149, for needle position when pivoting.) Sew around edges of each appliqué so that the straight stitches fall on the background fabric very near the appliqué and the "hem" stitches barely catch the folded edge of the appliqué (**Fig. 29**).

Fig. 29

6. It is not necessary to backstitch at the beginning or end of stitching. End stitching by sewing ¼" over the first stitches. Trim thread ends close to fabric.
7. To reduce bulk, turn project over and use scissors to cut away background (or other appliqué) fabric approximately ¼" inside stitching line of appliqué as shown in **Fig. 30**.

Fig. 30

wrong side

BORDERS

Borders cut along the lengthwise grain will lie flatter tha[n] borders cut along the crosswise grain. In most cases, our instructions for cutting borders for bed-size quilts includ[e] an extra 2" of length at each end for "insurance;" border[s] will be trimmed after measuring completed center section of quilt top.

ADDING SQUARED BORDERS

1. Mark the center of each edge of quilt top.
2. Squared borders are usually added to top and bottom, then side edges of the center section of quilt top. To add top and bottom borders, measure across center of quilt top to determine length of borders (**Fig. 31**). Trim top and bottom borders to the determined length.

Fig. 31

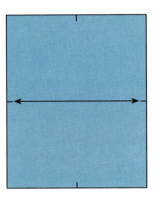

3. Mark center of 1 long edge of top border. Matching center marks and raw edges, pin border to quilt top, easing in any fullness; stitch[.] Repeat for bottom border.
4. Measure center of quilt top including attached borders to determine length of side borders. Trim side borders to the determined length. Repeat Step 3 to add borders to quilt top (**Fig. 32**[)].

Fig. 32

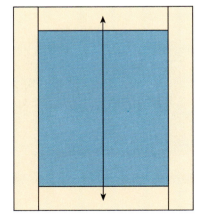

150

ADDING MITERED BORDERS

- Mark the center of each edge of quilt top.
- Mark center of 1 long edge of top border. Measure across center of quilt top (see **Fig. 31**). Matching center marks and raw edges, pin border to center of quilt top edge. From center of border, measure out ½ the width of the quilt top in both directions and mark. Match marks on border with corners of quilt top and pin. Easing in any fullness, pin border to quilt top between center and corners. Sew border to quilt top, beginning and ending seams **exactly** ¼" from each corner of quilt top and backstitching at beginning and end of stitching (**Fig. 33**).

Fig. 33

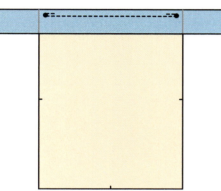

- Repeat Step 2 to sew bottom, then side borders, to center section of quilt top. To temporarily move first 2 borders out of the way, fold and pin ends as shown in **Fig. 34**.

Fig. 34

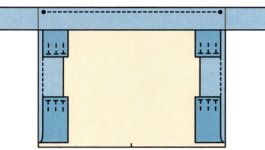

- Fold 1 corner of quilt top diagonally with right sides together and matching edges. Use ruler to mark stitching line as shown by pink line in **Fig. 35**. Pin borders together along drawn line. Sew on drawn line, backstitching at beginning and end of stitching (**Fig. 36**).

Fig. 35

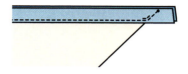

Fig. 36

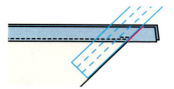

5. Turn mitered corner right side up. Check to make sure corner will lie flat with no gaps or puckers.
6. Trim seam allowance to ¼"; press to 1 side.
7. Repeat Steps 4 - 6 to miter each remaining corner.

QUILTING

Quilting holds the 3 layers (top, batting, and backing) of the quilt together and may be done by hand or machine. Our project instructions tell you which method is used on our quilts and show you quilting diagrams that can be used as suggestions for marking quilting designs. Because marking, layering, and quilting are interrelated and may be done in different orders depending on circumstances, please read this entire section, pages 151 - 154, before beginning the quilting process on your project.

TYPES OF QUILTING
In the Ditch
Quilting very close to a seamline (**Fig. 37**) or appliqué (**Fig. 38**) is called "in the ditch" quilting. This type of quilting does not need to be marked and is indicated on our quilting diagrams with blue lines close to seamlines. When quilting in the ditch, quilt on the side **opposite** the seam allowance.

Fig. 37

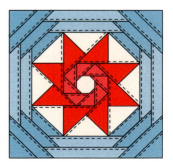

Fig. 38

Outline Quilting

Quilting approximately ¼" from a seam or appliqué is called "outline" quilting (**Fig. 39**). This type of quilting is indicated on our quilting diagrams by blue lines a short distance from seamlines. Outline quilting may be marked, or you may place ¼"w masking tape along seamlines and quilt along the opposite edge of the tape. (Do not leave tape on quilt longer than necessary, since it may leave an adhesive residue.)

Fig. 39

Ornamental Quilting

Quilting decorative lines or designs is called "ornamental" quilting (**Fig. 40**). Ornamental quilting is indicated on our quilting diagrams by blue lines. This type of quilting should be marked before you baste quilt layers together.

Fig. 40

MARKING QUILTING LINES

Fabric marking pencils, various types of chalk markers, and fabric marking pens with inks that disappear with exposure to air or water are readily available and work well for different applications. Graphite pencils work well on light-colored fabric, but marks may be difficult to remove. White pencils work well on dark-colored fabric, and silver pencils show up well on many colors. Since chalk rubs off easily, it's a good choice if you are marking as you quilt. Fabric marking pens make more durable and visible markings, but the marks may also be difficult to remove. Press down only as hard as necessary to make a visible line.

When you choose to mark your quilt, whether before or after the layers are basted together, is also a factor in deciding which marking tool to use. If you mark with chalk or a chalk pencil, handling the quilt during basting may rub off the markings. Intricate or ornamental designs may not be practical to mark as you quilt; mark these designs before basting using a more durable marker.

To choose marking tools, take all these factors into consideration and **test** different markers **on scrap fabric** until you find the one that gives the desired result.

USING QUILTING STENCILS

A wide variety of pre-cut quilting stencils, as well as entire books of quilting patterns, are available at your local quilt shop or fabric store. Our book includes pattern of some original quilting designs and some classics you might like to use on your project. Wherever you draw your quilting inspiration from, using a stencil makes it easier to mark intricate or repetitive designs on your quilt top.

1. To make a stencil from a pattern, center template plastic over pattern and use a permanent marker to trace pattern onto plastic.
2. Use a craft knife with a single or double blade to cut narrow slits along traced lines (**Fig. 41**).

Fig. 41

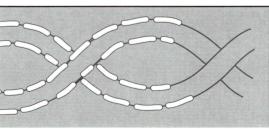

3. Use desired marking tool and stencil to mark quilting lines.

CHOOSING AND PREPARING THE BACKING

To allow for the quilt top shifting slightly during quilting, the backing should be approximately 4" larger on all sides for a bed-size quilt top or approximately 2" larger on all sides for a wall hanging. Yardage requirements listed for quilt backings are calculated for 45"w fabric. If you are making a bed-size quilt, using 90"w or 108"w fabric for the backing may eliminate piecing. To piece a backing using 45"w fabric, use the following instructions.

Measure length and width of quilt top; add 8" (4" for a wall hanging) to each measurement. If quilt top is 76"w or less, cut backing fabric into 2 lengths slightly longer than the determined **length** measurement. Trim selvages. Place lengths with right sides facing and sew long edges together, forming a tube (**Fig. 42**). Match seams and press along 1 fold (**Fig. 43**). Cut along pressed fold to form a single piece (**Fig. 44**).

Fig. 42   **Fig. 43**   **Fig. 44**

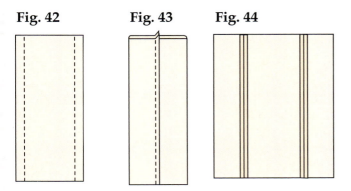

If quilt top is more than 76"w, cut backing fabric into 3 lengths slightly longer than the determined **width** measurement. Trim selvages. Sew long edges together to form a single piece. Trim backing to correct size, if necessary, and press seam allowances open.

CHOOSING AND PREPARING THE BATTING

Choosing the right batting will make your quilting job easier. For fine hand quilting, choose a low-loft batting in any of the fiber types described below. Machine quilters will want to choose a low-loft batting that is all cotton or a cotton/polyester blend because the cotton helps "grip" the layers of the quilt. If the quilt is to be tied, a high-loft batting, sometimes called extra-loft or fat batting, is a good choice.

Batting is available in many different fibers. Bonded polyester batting is one of the most popular batting types. It is treated with a protective coating to stabilize the fibers and to reduce "bearding," a process where batting fibers work their way out through the quilt fabrics. Other batting options include cotton/polyester batting, which combines the best of both polyester and cotton battings; all cotton batting, which must be quilted more closely than polyester batting; and wool or silk battings, which are generally more expensive and are usually only dry-cleanable.

Whichever batting you choose, read the manufacturer's instructions closely for any special notes on care or preparation. When you're ready to use your chosen batting in a project, cut the batting the same size as the prepared backing.

LAYERING THE QUILT

1. Examine wrong side of quilt top closely and trim any seam allowances and clip any threads that may show through the front of the quilt. Press quilt top.
2. If quilt top is to be marked before layering, mark quilting lines (see **Marking Quilting Lines**, page 152).
3. Place backing **wrong** side up on a flat surface. Use masking tape to tape edges of backing to surface. Place batting on wrong side of backing fabric. Smooth batting gently, being careful not to stretch or tear. Center quilt top **right** side up on batting.
4. If hand quilting, begin in the center and work toward the outer edges to hand baste all layers together. Use long stitches and place basting lines approximately 4" apart (**Fig. 45**). Smooth fullness or wrinkles toward outer edges.

Fig. 45

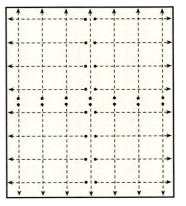

5. If machine quilting, use 1" rust-proof safety pins to "pin-baste" all layers together, spacing pins approximately 4" apart. Begin at the center and work toward the outer edges to secure all layers. If possible, place pins away from areas that will be quilted, although pins may be removed as needed when quilting.

HAND QUILTING

The quilting stitch is a basic running stitch that forms a broken line on the quilt top and backing. Stitches on the quilt top and backing should be straight and equal in length.

1. Secure center of quilt in hoop or frame. Check quilt top and backing to make sure they are smooth. To help prevent puckers, always begin quilting in the center of the quilt and work toward the outside edges.
2. Thread needle with an 18" - 20" length of quilting thread; knot 1 end. Using a thimble, insert needle into quilt top and batting approximately 1/2" from where you wish to begin quilting. Bring needle up at the point where you wish to begin (**Fig. 46**); when knot catches on quilt top, give thread a quick, short pull to "pop" knot through fabric into batting (**Fig. 47**).

Fig. 46

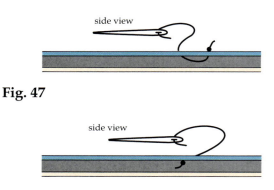
side view

Fig. 47

side view

3. Holding the needle with your sewing hand and placing your other hand underneath the quilt, use thimble to push the tip of the needle straight down through all layers. As soon as needle touches your finger underneath, use that finger to push only the tip of the needle back up through the layers to top of quilt. (The amount of the needle showing above the fabric determines the length of the quilting stitch.) Referring to **Fig. 48**, rock the needle up and down, taking 3 - 6 stitches before bringing the needle and thread completely through the layers. Check the back of the quilt to make sure stitches are going through all layers. When quilting through a seam allowance or quilting a curve or corner, you may need to take 1 stitch at a time.

Fig. 48

4. When you reach the end of your thread, knot thread close to the fabric and "pop" knot into batting; clip thread close to fabric.
5. Stop and move your hoop as often as necessary. You do not have to tie a knot every time you move your hoop; you may leave the thread dangling and pick it up again when you return to that part of the quilt.

MACHINE QUILTING

The machine-quilted projects in this book feature straight line quilting, which requires a walking foot or even-feed foot. The term "straight-line" is somewhat deceptive, since curves (especially gentle ones) as well as straight lines can be stitched using this technique.

1. Wind your sewing machine bobbin with general purpose thread that matches the quilt backing. Do not use quilting thread. Thread the needle on your machine with transparent monofilament thread if you want your quilting to blend with your quilt top fabrics. Use decorative thread, such as a metallic or contrasting colored general purpose thread, when you want the quilting lines to stand out more. Set the stitch length for 6 - 10 stitches per inch and attach the walking foot to sewing machine.
2. After pin-basting, decide which section of the quilt will have the longest continuous quilting line — oftentimes the area from center top to center bottom. Leaving the area exposed where you will place your first line of quilting, roll up each edge of the quilt to help reduce the bulk, keeping fabrics smooth. Smaller projects may not need to be rolled.
3. Start stitching at beginning of longest quilting line, using very short stitches for the first 1/4" to "lock" beginning of quilting line. Stitch across project, using one hand on each side of the walking foot to slightly spread the fabric and to guide the fabric through the machine. Lock stitches at end of quilting line.
4. Continue machine quilting, stitching the longer quilting lines first to stabilize the quilt before moving on to other areas.

BINDING

Binding encloses the raw edges of your quilt. Because of its stretchiness, bias binding works well for binding projects with curves or rounded corners; it also tends to lie smooth and flat in any given circumstance. Binding may also be cut from the straight lengthwise or crosswise grain of the fabric. You will find that straight-grain binding works well for projects with straight edges.

MAKING CONTINUOUS BIAS STRIP BINDING

Bias strips for binding can simply be cut and pieced to the desired length. However, when a long length of binding is needed, the "continuous" method is quick and accurate.

Cut a square from binding fabric the size indicated in the project instructions. Cut square in half diagonally to make 2 triangles. With right sides together and using a 1/4" seam allowance, sew triangles together (**Fig. 49**); press seam allowance open.

Fig. 49

On wrong side of fabric, draw lines the width of the binding as specified in the project instructions, usually 2 1/2" (**Fig. 50**). Cut off any remaining fabric less than this width.

Fig. 50

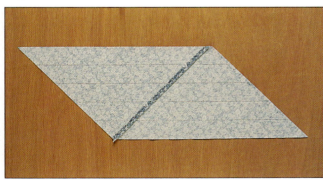

4. With right sides inside, bring short edges together to form a tube; match raw edges so that first drawn line of top section meets second drawn line of bottom section (**Fig. 51**). Carefully pin edges together by inserting pins through drawn lines at the point where drawn lines intersect, making sure the pins go through intersections on both sides. Using a 1/4" seam allowance, sew edges together. Press seam allowance open.

Fig. 51

5. To cut continuous strip, begin cutting along first drawn line (**Fig. 52**). Continue cutting along drawn line around tube.

Fig. 52

6. Trim ends of bias strip square.
7. Matching wrong sides and raw edges, press bias strip in half lengthwise to complete binding.

MAKING STRAIGHT-GRAIN BINDING

1. To determine length of strip needed if attaching binding with mitered corners, measure edges of the quilt and add 12".
2. To determine lengths of strips needed if attaching binding with overlapped corners, measure each edge of quilt; add 3" to each measurement.
3. Cut lengthwise or crosswise strips of binding fabric the determined length and the width called for in the project instructions. Strips may be pieced to achieve the necessary length.
4. Matching wrong sides and raw edges, press strip(s) in half lengthwise to complete binding.

ATTACHING BINDING WITH MITERED CORNERS

1. Press 1 end of binding diagonally (**Fig. 53**).

Fig. 53

2. Lay binding around quilt to make sure that seams in binding will not end up at a corner. Adjust placement if necessary. Matching raw edges of binding to raw edge of quilt top and beginning with pressed end several inches from a corner, pin binding to right side of quilt along 1 edge.
3. When you reach the first corner, mark ¹⁄₄" from corner of quilt (**Fig. 54**).

Fig. 54

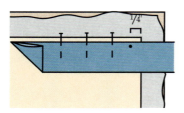

4. Using a ¹⁄₄" seam allowance, sew binding to quilt, backstitching at beginning of stitching and when you reach the mark (**Fig. 55**). Lift needle out of fabric and clip threads.

Fig. 55

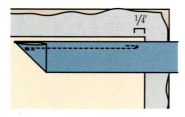

5. Fold binding as shown in **Figs. 56** and **57** and pin binding to adjacent side, matching raw edges. When you reach the next corner, mark ¹⁄₄" from edge of quilt.

Fig. 56   **Fig. 57**

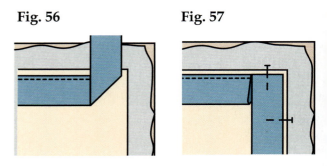

6. Backstitching at edge of quilt, sew pinned binding to quilt (**Fig. 58**); backstitch when you reach the next mark. Lift needle out of fabric and clip threads.

Fig. 58

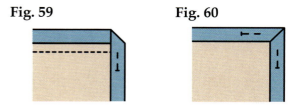

7. Repeat Steps 5 and 6 to continue sewing binding to quilt until binding overlaps beginning end by approximately 2". Trim excess binding.
8. If using 2¹⁄₂"w binding (finished size ¹⁄₂"), trim backing and batting a scant ¹⁄₄" larger than quilt top so that batting and backing will fill the binding when it is folded over to the quilt backing. If using narrower binding, trim backing and batting even with edges of quilt top.
9. On 1 edge of quilt, fold binding over to quilt backing and pin pressed edge in place, covering stitching line (**Fig. 59**). On adjacent side, fold binding over, forming a mitered corner (**Fig. 60**). Repeat to pin remainder of binding in place.

Fig. 59   **Fig. 60**

10. Blindstitch binding to backing.

ATTACHING BINDING WITH OVERLAPPED CORNERS

Matching raw edges and using a ¼" seam allowance, sew a length of binding to top and bottom edges on right side of quilt.
If using 2½"w binding (finished size ½"), trim backing and batting from top and bottom edges a scant ¼" larger than quilt top so that batting and backing will fill the binding when it is folded over to the quilt backing. If using narrower binding, trim backing and batting even with edges of quilt top.
Trim ends of binding even with edges of quilt top. Fold binding over to quilt backing and pin pressed edges in place, covering stitching line (**Fig. 61**); blindstitch binding to backing.

Fig. 61

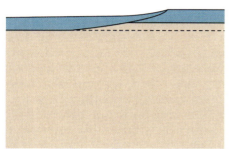

Leaving approximately 1½" of binding at each end, stitch a length of binding to each side edge of quilt. Trim backing and batting as in Step 2. Trim each end of binding ½" longer than bound edge. Fold each end of binding over to quilt backing (**Fig. 62**); pin in place. Fold binding over to quilt backing and blindstitch in place.

Fig. 62

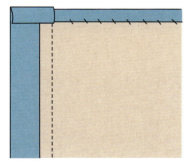

MAKING A HANGING SLEEVE

Attaching a hanging sleeve to the back of your wall hanging or quilt before the binding is added allows you to display your completed project on a wall.

1. Measure the width of the wall hanging top and subtract 1". Cut a piece of fabric 7"w by the determined measurement.
2. Press short edges of fabric piece ¼" to wrong side; press edges ¼" to wrong side again and machine stitch in place.
3. Matching wrong sides, fold piece in half lengthwise to form a tube.
4. Follow project instructions to sew binding to quilt top and to trim backing and batting. Before blindstitching binding to backing, match raw edges and stitch hanging sleeve to center top edge on back of wall hanging.
5. Finish binding wall hanging, treating the hanging sleeve as part of the backing.
6. Blindstitch bottom of hanging sleeve to backing, taking care not to stitch through to front of quilt.
7. Insert dowel or slat into hanging sleeve.

SIGNING AND DATING YOUR QUILT

Your completed quilt is a work of art and should be treated as such. And like any artist, you should sign and date your work. There are many different ways to do this, and you should pick a method of signing and dating that reflects the quilt, the occasion for which it was made, and your own particular talents.

The following suggestions may give you an idea for recording the history of your quilt for future generations.

- Embroider your name, the date, and any additional information on the quilt top or backing. You may use floss colors that closely match the fabric you are working on, such as white floss on a white border, or contrasting colors may be used.
- Make a label from muslin and use a permanent marker to write your information. Your label may be as plain or as fancy as you wish. Then stitch the label to the back of the quilt.
- Chart a cross-stitch label design that includes the information you wish and stitch it in colors that complement the quilt. Stitch the finished label to the quilt backing.

PILLOW FINISHING

Any quilt block may be made into a pillow. If desired, you may add welting and/or a ruffle to the pillow top before adding the backing.

ADDING WELTING TO PILLOW TOP

1. To make welting, measure edges of pillow top and add 4". Cut a bias strip of fabric the width specified in project instructions, equal in length to determined measurement, piecing if necessary.
2. Lay cord along center of bias strip on wrong side of fabric; fold strip over cord. Using a zipper foot, machine baste along length of strip close to cord. Trim seam allowance to the width you will use to sew pillow top and back together (see Step 2 of **Making the Pillow**).
3. Matching raw edges and beginning and ending 3" from ends of welting, baste welting to right side of pillow top. To make turning corners easier, clip seam allowance of welting at pillow top corners.
4. Remove approximately 3" of seam at 1 end of welting; fold fabric away from cord. Trim remaining end of welting so that cord ends meet exactly. Fold short edge of welting fabric 1/2" to wrong side; fold fabric back over area where ends meet (**Fig. 63**). Baste remainder of welting to pillow top close to cord.

Fig. 63

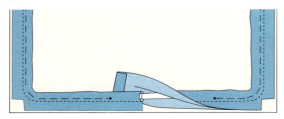

5. Follow **Making the Pillow** to complete pillow.

ADDING RUFFLE TO PILLOW TOP

1. To determine length of ruffle fabric, measure edges of pillow top and multiply by 2. To determine width of ruffle fabric, multiply the finished width measurement given in project instructions by 2. Add 1" to width measurement if using a 1/2" seam allowance to complete pillow or 1/2" to measurement if using a 1/4" seam allowance (see Step 2 of **Making the Pillow**). Cut a strip of fabric the determined measurements, piecing if necessary.
2. Matching right sides, use a 1/4" seam allowance to sew short edges of ruffle together to form a large circle; press seam allowance open. To fold ruffle in half, match raw edges and fold 1 raw edge of fabric to inside of circle to meet remaining raw edge of fabric; press.

3. To gather ruffle, place quilting thread 1/4" from raw edge of ruffle. Using a medium width zigzag stitch with medium stitch length, stitch over quilting thread, being careful not to catch quilting thread in stitching. Pull quilting thread, drawing up gathers to fit pillow top.
4. Matching raw edges, baste ruffle to right side of pillow top.
5. Follow **Making the Pillow** to complete pillow.

MAKING THE PILLOW

1. For pillow back, cut a piece of fabric the same size as pieced and quilted pillow top.
2. Place pillow back and pillow top right sides together. The seam allowance width you use will depend on the construction of the pillow top. If the pillow top has borders where the finished width of the border is not crucial, use a 1/2" seam allowance for durability. If the pillow top is pieced where a wider seam allowance would interfere with the design, use a 1/4" seam allowance. Using the determined seam allowance (or stitching as close as possible to welting), sew pillow top and back together, leaving an opening at bottom edge for turning.
3. Turn pillow right side out, carefully pushing corners outward. Stuff with polyester fiberfill or pillow form and sew final closure by hand.

STENCILING

1. To make stencil, use a permanent marker to trace pattern onto plastic template material; cut out design with craft knife.
2. Place stencil in position on right side of fabric. Dip brush in paint and remove excess on paper towel. Brush should be almost dry. Apply paint in a stamping motion to fill in design area. Carefully remove stencil and allow to dry. Reposition stencil as necessary to complete stenciling.

QUILTING GLOSSARY

Appliqué — A cutout fabric shape that is secured to a larger background. Also refers to the technique of securing the cutout pieces.

Backing — The back or bottom layer of a quilt, sometimes called the "lining."

Backstitch — A reinforcing stitch taken at the beginning and end of a seam to secure stitches.

Basting — Large running stitches used to temporarily secure pieces or layers of fabric together. Basting is removed after permanent stitching.

Batting — The middle layer of a quilt that provides the insulation and warmth as well as the thickness.

as — The diagonal (45° for true bias) grain of fabric in relation to crosswise or lengthwise grain (see **Fig. 64**).

nding — The fabric strip used to enclose the raw edges of the layered and quilted quilt. Also refers to the technique of finishing quilt edges in this way.

indstitch — A nearly invisible hand stitch used to sew binding to a quilt backing or to close an opening on a pillow.

order — Strips of fabric that are used to frame a quilt top.

hain piecing — A machine-piecing method consisting of joining pairs of pieces one after the other by feeding them through the sewing machine without cutting the thread between the pairs.

rain — The direction of the threads in woven fabric. "Crosswise grain" refers to the threads running from selvage to selvage. "Lengthwise grain" refers to the threads running parallel to the selvages (**Fig. 64**).

Fig. 64

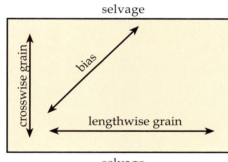

selvage

crosswise grain

bias

lengthwise grain

selvage

achine baste — To baste using a sewing machine set at a long stitch length.

iter — A method used to finish corners of quilt borders or bindings, consisting of joining fabric pieces at a 45° angle.

ecing — Sewing together the pieces of a quilt design to form a quilt block or an entire quilt top.

n basting — Using rust-proof safety pins to pin the layers of a quilt together prior to quilting.

uilt block — Pieced or appliquéd sections that are sewn together to form a quilt top.

uilt top — The decorative part of a quilt that is layered on top of the batting and backing.

uilting — The stitching that holds together the 3 quilt layers (top, batting, and backing); or, the entire process of making a quilt.

Running stitch — A series of straight stitches with the stitch length equal to the space between stitches (**Fig. 65**).

Fig. 65

Sashing — Strips or blocks of fabric that separate individual blocks in a quilt top.

Seam allowance — The distance between the seam and the cut edge of the fabric. In quilting, the seam allowance is usually 1/4".

Selvages — The 2 finished lengthwise edges of fabric (see **Fig. 64**). Selvages should be trimmed from fabric before cutting.

Set (or Setting) — The arrangement of the quilt blocks as they are sewn together to form the quilt top.

Setting squares — Squares of plain (unpieced) fabric set between pieced or appliquéd quilt blocks in a quilt top.

Setting triangles — Triangles of fabric used around the outside of a diagonally-set quilt top to fill in between outer squares and border or binding.

Stencil — A pattern used for marking quilting lines.

Straight grain — The crosswise or lengthwise grain of fabric (see **Fig. 64**). The lengthwise grain has the least amount of stretch.

Strip set — Two or more strips of fabric that are sewn together along the long edges and then cut apart across the width of the sewn strips to create smaller units.

Template — A pattern used for marking quilt pieces to be cut out.

Triangle-square — In piecing, 2 right triangles joined along their long sides to form a square with a diagonal seam (**Fig. 66**).

Fig. 66

Unit — A pieced section that is made as individual steps in the quilt construction process are completed. Units are usually combined to make blocks or other sections of the quilt top.

CREDITS

We want to extend a warm *thank you* to the generous people who allowed us to photograph our projects at their homes.

- *Star-Bright Collection:* August and Christy Myers
- *Burgoyne Surrounded:* Nancy Gunn Porter
- *Soft & Sweet Pillows:* Carol Clawson
- *O My Stars! Collection:* Bill and Nancy Appleton
- *Dresden Plate:* Gail Wilcox
- *Flying Geese:* Dr. Tony Johnson
- *Pastel Posies Collection:* Ron and Bobbie McKenzie
- *Colorado Log Cabin:* Dick and Joan Rechtin
- *Old Maid's Puzzle:* Dick and Joan Rechtin
- *All-American Collection:* Dr. David and Linda Smith
- *Springtime Baby Quilt:* Becky Thompson
- *Autumn Blooms Collection:* Nancy Gunn Porter
- *Country Chickens Collection:* Carol Clawson
- *Quilter's Christmas Collection:* Dr. Tony Johnson

We also thank Ethan Allen Home Interiors, Little Rock, Arkansas, for allowing us to photograph our *Robbing Peter to Pay Paul* quilt in the store.

The following projects are from the collection of Bryce and Donna Hamilton, Minneapolis, Minnesota: Dresden Plate quilt, page 48; Flying Geese quilt, page 54; Colorado Log Cabin quilt, page 70; and Schoolhouse wall hanging, page 84. Designs from the Hamiltons' collection also inspired the O My Stars! quilt, page 28, and the Feathered Star wall hanging, page 30.

The projects in the *Country Chickens Collection* were designed by Mary Tendall and Connie Tesene of Country Threads, Inc.®, Garner, Iowa 50438.

To Magna IV Color Imaging of Little Rock, Arkansas, we say thank you for the superb color reproduction and excellent pre-press preparation.

We especially want to thank photographers Mark Mathews, Larry Pennington, Karen Shirey, and Ken West of Peerless Photography, Little Rock, Arkansas, and Jerry R. Davis of Jerry Davis Photography, Little Rock, Arkansas, for their time, patience, and excellent work.

We extend a sincere *thank you* to all the people who assisted in making and testing the projects in this book: Karen Call; Debbie Chance; Nora Faye Clift; Cindy Davis; Stephanie Fite; Elise Frahm; Patricia Galas; Genny Garrett; Judith Hassed; Shirley Howton; Judith Kline; Barbara Middleton; Ruby Solida; Leon Stout; Glenda Taylor; Karen Tyler; members of the Gardner Memorial United Methodist Church, North Little Rock, Arkansas: Elois Allain, Phula Barnett, Maxie Bramblett, Ruth Chronister, Leon Dickey, Alice Dong, Vina Lendermon, Fredda McBride, Edna Sikes, Betty Smith, Esther Starkey, and Thelma Starkey; members of the Highland Valley United Methodist Church, Little Rock, Arkansas: Frieda Bard, Thelma Bouton, Blanche Hicks, Jean Hooper, Ethil Martin, Joyce May, Velma Shaneyfelt, Lucile Shivley, and Ida Marie Sisco; and members of the First Assembly of God Church Women's Ministries, Searcy, Arkansas: Frances Blackburn, Wanda Fite, Bonnie Gowan, Juanita Hodges, Minnie Hogan, Ida Johnson, Ruby Johnson, Richadeen Lewis, Velrie Louks, Sammie McDonald, and Minnie Whitehurst.